CONTENTS

1
Introducing California

Ever since it was besieged by the **49ers** of the gold rush, California has been the promised land: a place where dreams come true and where limitless wealth and opportunity can be acquired just by turning up. Plenty of people still do turn up – be they would-be **film stars** or **migrant farm labourers** – in the pursuit of riches and fame, or just a better life, even though they know that California's reality lags way behind the myth.

California has more people and a bigger economy than most countries, and has given the world such remarkable innovations as drive-in churches, mountain bikes, and personal computers. But coupled to the highly visible wealth and prosperity is another California of poverty, gang-rivalry and inter-ethnic tension. Underlying economic problems were overshadowed by a booming dotcom sector through the 1990s, but the subsequent bust contributed to the election of actor Arnold Schwarzenegger as Governer in 2003.

For travellers, though, California really does have the potential to fulfil their greatest expectations. You can **ski** and **surf** on the same day, tour fine **museums** and eat **gourmet food** to your heart's content. Although climate dictates that it would take a year to see it all, the state has everything from parched **deserts** to **snow-capped mountains** – often within sight of one another, deep **forests** in which stand the world's tallest trees, and a lengthy coastline that varies from the surfer-dominated sands of the south to the wet and windy headlands of the north.

*** San Francisco: probably the most beautiful city in the USA.
*** Disneyland®: greatest theme park in the world.
*** Yosemite National Park: from the valley to the back-country, natural California at its most pristine and spectacular.
** Death Valley National Park: unforgettable landscapes in the USA's lowest, driest, hottest place.
* Hearst Castle: an overstated monument to one man's vast wealth.

Opposite: *California has cult status among surfers.*

The coastal south experiences mild winters and hot summers with most rainfall through the winter. The Gold Country and Sierra Nevada see heavy winter snowfalls and generally mild, dry summers. San Francisco has a mild year-round climate but, especially during summer, is cooled by morning and evening fogs. Fog is also common along the northern coast, where only a short, dry summer brings respite from heavy rain. The inland north has freezing winters and sunny, mild summers.

THE LAND

Filling 158,693 sq miles (411,122km²), California is the third-largest state in the USA and, with 37 million people, is the most populous. The state averages 780 miles (1255km) in length and is between 150 miles (242km) and 350 miles (563km) in width.

Climate

A combination of mountains, ocean and deserts gives California a climate of extremes. In the south, cities such as **Los Angeles** and **San Diego** claim the best of the state's beaches and a climate conforming to the popular image of California as a place of surfing and sunshine.

Along the **Central Coast** and **Northern Coast** temperatures are considerably lower and fog is common. Summers in **San Francisco**, the north's major city, are chilled by morning and evening fog. With some sections receiving around 80 inches (2030mm) annually, the northern coast has the highest rainfall in the contiguous USA, most falling between October and March. In the same region, **Point Reyes National Seashore** has the coolest mid-summers in the continental USA.

The inland valleys generally have warmer, drier conditions though here, too, weather can vary over a short distance. Such 'micro-climate' conditions are important to vintners in California's **Wine Country**, which occupies just two small valleys some 40 miles (64km) north of San Francisco.

California's mountains, particularly the **Sierra Nevada**, have some of the heaviest snowfalls in the USA, usually beginning in late autumn and lasting until spring. To the east of the Sierra Nevada lie the **desert regions**, where summer temperatures have reached 134°F (57°C) in the shade and where rainfall is rare and can fall as flash floods. These severe conditions have given rise to sights of spectacular beauty, such as **Death Valley** and **Joshua Tree** national parks, as well as oases occupied by wealthy towns such as **Palm Springs**.

Below: *Created by wind action over thousands of years, the sand dunes of Death Valley.*

Mountains and Rivers

California's regions are defined by mountain ranges. The Sierra Nevada divides the arid desert regions from the fertile 20,000-sq-mile (51,814km²) Central Valley. On their eastern side, the mountains rise stark and sharp above the deserts; their gentle western slopes hold dense forests.

The **Coastal Ranges** form the Central Valley's western edge and continue to the ocean, creating the wild vistas of the Central Coast. The **Cascade Mountains** are a northerly continuation of the Sierra Nevada and reach into northeast California. Adjoining the Cascades in northwest California, the **Klamath Mountains** have coastal slopes sufficiently damp and foggy to support groves of redwoods.

The sunny, pleasant conditions of Southern California are due to a south-facing coast (much of the rest faces west), and the influence of the east – west running Transverse Ranges; mountains which divide Los Angeles from the Central Valley and continue into the desert.

All of California's major rivers are in the north, the largest being the 400-mile-long (644km) **Sacramento River**. Diverting rivers to move freshwater south is the source of much environmental and political controversy within the state (see p. 8).

- **Area:** 158,693 sq miles (411,122km²), third largest US state.
- **Highest Point:** Mount Whitney, 14,494ft (4418m).
- **Lowest Point:** Badwater, Death Valley, 282ft (86m) below sea level.
- **Coastline:** 1264 miles (2034km) in length.
- **Population:** 37 million, projected to reach 50 million by 2025. California is the USA's most populous state – more residents than Canada.
- **National Parks:** 22, including national monuments, national historic sites and national recreational areas.
- **State Parks:** 270, including state beaches, historical parks and a historic monument.

Above: *The Sierra Nevada mountains seen from the arid east.*
Below: *Yosemite National Park, part of the Sierra Nevada. Covered in snow, it is natural California at its best.*

Above: *Spanish Bay on the Monterey Peninsula is a tranquil retreat from the hustle and bustle.*

Seas and Shores

Of California's 1264 miles (2034km) of coast, only the southern quarter fulfils the popular expectation of sun-drenched sands. Between **Santa Barbara** and the US-Mexico border, most **beaches** are broad, sandy and sunny, and often packed with surfers and sunbathers.

These are beaches where **swimming** is generally safe, though you should check that a lifeguard is present (indicated by signs). Elsewhere, the ocean is usually too dangerous or simply too cold, though **Stinson Beach**, just north of San Francisco, and **Santa Cruz** are notable exceptions to the norm.

Legally, almost all the Californian coast is publicly owned and many sections are specifically protected by the state, either as state beaches – often with picnic facilities – or as parks and reserves for wildlife, such as **Point Lobos State Reserve** near Carmel. Low tide along the shoreline often reveals **tidepools**, some of the most interesting are at **Point Loma**, in San Diego, and at **Point Reyes National Seashore**, on the northern coast.

Traditionally, digging for clams (especially at **Pismo Beach**, on the Central Coast) has been a coastal pastime but, to preserve stocks, this activity is now permitted only on a few weekends each year.

Two of California's most spectacular bodies of water are inland. Spanning 200 sq miles (520km²), **Lake Tahoe**, in the Sierra Nevada, is the US's largest alpine lake. In the Eastern Sierra, the intensely alkaline **Mono Lake** is

---

Northern California's Water

The dependence of Southern California on Northern California's water – 70% of the state's rivers are in the north while 80% of the demand for fresh water is in the south – led to widespread damming of northern rivers. Consequently, San Francisco Bay has become increasingly saline and less able to support the migratory birdlife which depends on it. Falling water levels in **Mono Lake**, caused by the moving of fresh water 200 miles (322km) south to Los Angeles, has caused ecological disturbance in the Eastern Sierra.

of great ecological importance, not least as a breeding ground for gulls. However, the lake's level has fallen over 40ft (12m) since 1941, when its feeder streams were first diverted south, adversely affecting the wildlife dependent upon it. The same process has exposed dramatic tufa formations.

Earthquakes and Volcanic Activity

California sits on the unstable meeting point of the Pacific and North American plates. Hundreds of geological fault lines lie beneath the state, the largest being the 600-mile (975km) **San Andreas** fault which on average experiences a quake large enough to be felt every three days. California is thought to have experienced 18,000 quakes above magnitude three on the Richter Scale since 1808.

The majority of Californian earthquakes do not adversely affect people or property, being too weak or occurring far from populated areas. However, experts predict that a highly destructive earthquake, magnitude 8 or more, will strike a densely populated area within the next 30 years.

Volcanic activity is another result of California's unstable geology, although the last major eruption occurred in 1915 and no more are expected in the foreseeable future. The 1915 eruption took place at **Mount Lassen** in the Far North. The area's continuing geothermal activity, such as bubbling pits of mud and sulphur vents, is visible at **Lassen Volcanic National Park**.

Evidence of prehistoric volcanic activity lies all over California and includes the lava caves of the Far North's **Lava Beds National Park**, the basalt columns of the Eastern Sierra's **Devil's Postpile Monument**, and the Wine Country's **Old Faithful Geyser**. Geothermal hot springs are common throughout the mountain regions.

EARTHQUAKE SAFETY

Statistically, visitors are extremely unlikely to be adversely affected by a Californian earthquake though they may well experience a mild one. If a major quake should strike during your visit, there are a few basics tips worth heeding.

If indoors, **stand in a doorway:** the frame will provide some protection if the rest of the building collapses. If outdoors, keep clear of glass falling from the windows of tall buildings. Telephone books carry further safety tips.

Below: *A section of the San Andreas Fault.*

Distinguished by its twisted, upturned branches and spiky fruit, the Joshua tree is found across California's desert regions at altitudes of 3000–5000ft (914–1524m), with the most spectacular examples in the **Joshua Tree National Park**. The Joshua tree is actually a plant, a species of giant yucca, and can reach 50ft (15m) in height.

Below: *A giant sequoia of Yosemite National Park's Mariposa Grove.*

Plant Life

Native to California are 260 bird species, 54 types of cactus, 5200 plants (1500 of which are endemic), and over 27,000 types of insect – all part of a natural cornucopia that includes everything from the world's tallest trees to a desert-dwelling fish.

The fogs and heavy rainfall of the northern Californian coast are ideal conditions for the **coastal redwood**, the world's tallest tree, growing up to 367ft (112m). The redwoods' shallow roots make the trees susceptible to high winds and for mutual protection they grow in tightly packed groves. The related **giant sequoia**, the world's largest living thing, is found in the foothills of the Sierra Nevada. The biggest giant sequoia measures 103ft (31m) in circumference.

In the arid conditions of the Eastern Sierra grow the world's oldest living trees: the 4000-year old **bristlecone pines**. The bristlecone pines may only grow one inch (25mm) a year but their widely spread root system enables any available moisture to be absorbed. The bristlecones are just one of over 20 different pine species found in California. The rarest is the **torrey pine**, growing in a single protected spot just north of San Diego.

Of California's 800 wildflowers, the **California poppy** is the state's official flower and grows in coastal regions. Desert regions are noted for their springtime wildflowers, when **primrose**, **verbena** and assorted **flowering cacti** bring colour to the desert floor.

Wildlife

Mountain foothills provide habitats for **black bear** (California's last wild grizzly bear was killed in 1922), deer, bobcats, foxes and raccoons, and the rarely sighted 3000 **mountain lions** estimated to live in more remote mountain areas. Also rarely sighted is the huge **California condor**, a black-plumed vulture extinct in the wild but recently reintroduced by a successful captive breeding programme.

Above: *A bald eagle, one of two types of eagle native to California.*

Desert denizens include large mammals such as the **big horn sheep**, occasionally glimpsed on hillsides, and smaller creatures such as the **desert tortoise**, the **kangaroo rat**, named for its hopping run, and the **red spotted toad**, able to cool its body temperature by absorbing its own urine. In the saline pools of Death Valley are 2 inch-long (50mm) **pup fish**. **Rattlesnakes**, **scorpions** and **black widow** spiders are also found; heed the warnings in the leaflets distributed at popular desert areas.

The **sea lions** encountered all along the coast are most likely to be Californian sea lions, although the larger stellar inhabits the coast north of Santa Barbara. Less common is the **elephant seal** of the northern coast. During December and January, elephant seals, which weigh up to 4 tonnes, gather to mate at Año Nuevo State Reserve, south of San Francisco.

From the marked whale-watching points dotted along the Californian coast, whales can often be seen on their annual migration between the months of December and March. Weighing up to 40 tonnes, gray whales are unique in feeding directly from the ocean floor, leaving indentations in the sea bed with their tongues.

In the arid conditions of the Eastern Sierra grow what are claimed to be the world's **oldest living trees**: the 4000-year-old bristlecone pines. In these adverse conditions, the bristlecone pines may only grow an inch a year but their widely spread root system enables any available moisture to be absorbed. The root system also prevents the trees growing close together, thereby reducing the risk of destruction by forest fire.

Above: *The seemingly truncated form of Half Dome, looking east from Glacier Point, Yosemite National Park.*

PLATE TECTONICS

California straddles the North American and the Pacific tectonic plates, two of the world's 20 tectonic plates which 'float' on semi-liquid rock deep beneath the earth's surface with the continents above them. Periodic release of the enormous pressures built up as the plates move in conflicting directions is the cause of California's earthquakes. Beneath California, the movement of the plates is slow but ceaseless: predictions suggest that LA will one day be further north than San Francisco.

HISTORY IN BRIEF

California and history might seem mutually exclusive terms, but even the briefest acquaintance with the state throws up plenty of evidence of the action-packed two centuries since it was first settled by Europeans – be it Spanish missions, gold-rush towns or the world's first freeways.

Formation

The earthquakes which are a feature of Californian life are a constant reminder that the state occupies a still active section of the earth's crust; the state's landscapes still being shaped by the release of huge underground pressures as the Pacific and North American tectonic plates collide and push against each other.

What became California was beneath the **Pacific Ocean** until the plates forced each other upwards to create immense underwater mountains, which rose above water around 25 million years ago.

About nine million years later, one group of mountains, later named the **Sierra Nevada**, became tall enough to prevent the passage of rain from the west. This eventually caused the area east of the mountains to become arid, evolving into the desert regions of present-day California.

Subsequently, several ice ages brought the glacial erosion which sculptured some of the state's most dramatic natural features, such as **Yosemite Valley** in Yosemite National Park. Rising ocean levels at the end of the last ice age, around 10,000 years ago, brought sea water flooding into inland valleys, among them that which became **San Francisco Bay**.

Native Peoples

At the time of European contact in the 18th century, 300,000 native people are believed to have been living in California, descendants of an Asian race thought to have crossed 6000–12,000 years ago from **Siberia** (then linked to Alaska by land). Despite their common ancestry, the California natives divided into 105 different ethnic groups, each following a particular belief system and speaking one of a hundred dialects derived from five root languages.

Acorns mashed into bread provided the staple diet for many native Californians but this was often augmented by fresh meat or fish, both of which were in plentiful supply to all but the desert-dwelling

Above: *Well-preserved petroglyphs discovered in the Mojave Desert.*

HISTORICAL CALENDAR

1533 First European sighting by Spanish explorers.
1542 First European landing in San Diego Bay.
1579 Francis Drake claims California for England.
1602 Spaniard Sebastián Vizcaíno maps and names coastal features.
1769 Spanish launch Sacred Expedition, founding the first mission at San Diego. First sighting of San Francisco Bay. First Californian earthquake to be experienced by Europeans.
1812 Russians establish a fur trapping settlement at Fort Ross.
1822 California officially becomes part of Mexico.
1834 Missions secularized.
1847 California formally becomes a US possession.
1848 Discovery of gold in the foothills of Sierra Nevada.

1850 California acquires statehood.
1857 First commercial winery established, in the Sonoma Valley.
1869 Completion of transcontinental railroad, linking California to the Eastern USA.
1897 Formation of Sierra Club, California's first conservation organization.
1906 Earthquake and fire destroys San Francisco.
1913 First full-length feature made in Hollywood: Cecil B DeMille's *The Squaw Man*.
1920 For the first time, the population of Los Angeles exceeds that of San Francisco.
1932 Olympic Games held in Los Angeles.
1933 Earthquake in Long Beach (Los Angeles) leads to new building safety codes.

1934 Four-day general strike in San Francisco, in protest against police shooting of two striking dockers.
1937 Golden Gate Bridge completed in San Francisco.
1955 Disneyland® opens.
1962 California becomes the nation's most populous state.
1965 Watts Riots in Los Angeles leave 36 dead.
1989 The Loma Prieta earthquake closes San Francisco's Bay Bridge for a month.
1992 The Rodney King riots in Los Angeles leave 58 dead.
1994 Earthquake in Los Angeles kills 33 and renders 20,000 homeless.
1998 Smoking is banned in bars, restaurants and clubs.
2001 Power cuts rock the state.
2004 San Francisco issues marriage licenses to same-sex couples.

California's native population had declined to 150,000 when the missions were secularized in 1834. White demand for land following the gold rush saw even greater numbers perish and only 17,000 remained in 1913. Not until the 1960s was there government acknowledgement of native claims for the return of land and financial compensation. The same period saw Native Americans become California's fastest-growing ethnic minority; their number reached 91,000 in 1970 and is now estimated at 330,000.

Missions were often built close to a *presidio* (garrison for troops), and generally comprised a church, library, living and dining quarters for priests, dormitories for natives, an infirmary, and workshops. Here, neophytes (as natives taken into missions were known) were taught rudimentary skills in building, wine making, spinning and tanning. By the time of ecularization, an estimated 88,000 natives had been baptized into the Catholic faith and 24,000 had undergone Catholic marriage ceremonies.

peoples. Although there was no communication between the native Californians on a wide scale, neighbouring groups did mix and trade with one another; rarely was there any conflict.

While the religious practices varied, the most powerful spiritual code was the *Kukso*, common in central California. A feature of *Kukso* was a ritual dance performed by initiated males wearing costumes representing spirits.

Among native Californians, artistic skills and cultural pride were expressed through handicrafts such as the highly decorative spoons carved from elk horn by the **Yurok** in the north, the elaborate basketry of the **Pomo** in central California, and the rock art of the **Chumash** further south, still visible near Santa Barbara.

European Discovery and Settlement

The peninsula of **Baja** (or 'lower') **California**, now part of Mexico, was first sighted by the Spaniard **Hernándo Cortés** in 1533. The first European landing in what is now the state of California was made by Portuguese navigator **Juan Cabrillo**, who dropped anchor in 1542 off what became San Diego. In 1579, **Francis Drake** put ashore in northern California for repairs and claimed the land for England. Meanwhile, **Russia** and **France** were viewing California with interest from fur-trapping settlements further north.

Not until about 200 years later, however, when California was found to be part of the North American mainland (previously it had been thought to be an island), were there efforts at settlement. Already established in South and Central America, the **Spanish** began the **Sacred Expedition** into California from **Mexico** in 1769. This resulted in the founding of 21 Spanish missions, from San Diego in the south to Sonoma in the north, each measured to be a day's horse ride from the next.

While the Spanish missions ostensibly had a religious purpose – to convert the natives to Catholicism – they were also intended to deter rival European powers and gain the loyalty of the natives, who provided manual labour. Importing cattle and growing food, many missions became self-sufficient and some became rich. For the native Californians, though, the European arrival presaged the end of their culture and the decimation of their population, mostly through lack of resistance to European-borne diseases.

The Mexican Era

California was an isolated outpost of the Spanish empire and regarded as unimportant, a view shared by Mexico which gained independence (and with it California) from Spain in 1822.

California became ruled by the **Californios**, California-born persons of Mexican or Spanish descent who acquired land as the Mexican government secularized the missions. Rich through land ownership and through selling cattle hides to US traders (who then manufactured leather goods to sell back to the Californios), a few distinguished Californio families dominated Californian life.

Generally more disposed towards a lively social life than conducting business, the Californios granted large land holdings to hard-working immigrants from Europe while a number of US citizens (banned from owning California land in their own name and generally viewed with suspicion as the USA steadily expanded its western boundaries) married into the leading families, thereby acquiring great wealth and influence.

US Acquisition

The doctrine of **Manifest Destiny**, a term coined in 1845 to describe the USA's moral right to spread across the continent, helped fuel the US-Mexico War which

In April 1846, a bedraggled group of fur trappers pre-empted the US annexation of California by entering the northern town of **Sonoma**, taking the surrender of the Mexican governor, declaring California an independent republic and hoisting the 'Bear Flag'. This situation lasted only until news arrived of the US capture of **Monterey** in July. Nonetheless, the bear in the California state flag represents the bear of the 1846 republic.

Below: *Mission San Miguel, north of San Luis Obispo was built in 1797 by Spanish missionaries.*

began the same year. The war led to the landing of US troops in California where they encountered little opposition. By July, 1846, every major California town was under US control and the following year the region formally became a US possession under Mexico's surrender terms.

The Gold Rush

On 28 January, 1848, a farm worker discovered flakes of gold in a river 50 miles (81km) east of **Sacramento**. Washed down slowly over millions of years from the gold-bearing foothills of the **Sierra Nevada** mountains, California gold was, to all intents and purposes, there for the taking. With communications within California and across the USA being unreliable, the news was slow to spread and many people simply did not believe it.

As the truth of the discovery became accepted, California was on the receiving end of one of the biggest movements of people the world had ever seen. Throughout 1849, the California gold rush brought tens of thousands of gold seekers – nicknamed the **49ers** – from the USA and elsewhere. Most arrived by ship, though some made the perilous overland journey from the American East. In just two years, San Francisco's population swelled from about 500 to 25,000; California's rising from about 7000 to 100,000 in four years.

With river-borne gold soon exhausted, the fortune hunters turned their attention to the hills in which the precious metal was buried. Mining companies quickly replaced the lone gold panner and jerry-built towns arose, housing the local mine's predominantly single male workforce and quickly earning a reputation for lawlessness, gambling and heavy drinking.

Below: *The much-restored buildings of Old Town Sacramento provide a highly cleansed impression of gold rush-era California.*

In the peak year of 1852, California's mines yielded gold worth $81 million, confirming the transformation of the region from distant and quiet outpost to an economically powerful state.

Railroads and the First California Millionaires

Gold-rush fortunes were made less by miners than by the merchants who supplied them with equipment.

Above: *The former gold-mining town now preserved as Bodie State Historic Park.*

Four such merchants – Charles Crocker, Mark Hopkins, Collis P. Huntington and Leland Stanford – became known as the **Big Four** as they acquired still greater wealth through ownership of the **Central Pacific Railroad Company**.

The Big Four dishonestly acquired federal grants as they built the tracks which formed the western leg of the transcontinental railroad, the first fixed link between California and the American East and completed in 1869. With many Californian towns dependent on the railroad for their survival, the Big Four were able to acquire unprecedented political power and amass vast fortunes.

As the Big Four lavished some of their money on elaborate mansions in San Francisco's exclusive **Nob Hill** district, they seemed impervious to the economic decline wrought by the end of the gold rush and by the flood of cheap goods from the east on the railroad, which put many local traders out of business.

Public opprobrium for the depression was unfairly directed at **the Chinese**, around 10,000 of whom had worked on the Big Four's railroad and who, by 1872,

Conventional history has it that California's first **Chinese** arrived during the gold rush (California having been dubbed 'Gold Mountain' in **Cantonese**). Recent finds on the coast near Los Angeles may cause the history books to be rewritten, however, suggesting that Chinese seafarers may have landed many years earlier. The claim appears to be supported by documents discovered in China apparently describing an accidental Chinese landing in California around **217BC**.

Above: *A stunning Victorian San Francisco home on Alamo Square.*

Through the 1920s, fast-growing Los Angeles became the first city to be planned for the car, its suburbs being linked to the city centre by a network of freeways – the first opening in 1940. Dependence on the car would bring the city considerable environmental problems. The city had its first official smog alert in 1943 and, currently, Angelenos collectively drive 295.5 million miles a day. Unsurprisingly, vehicle emissions are the major contributor to the city's pollution problems.

held half the factory jobs in San Francisco. Legalized racism resulted in the Chinese being confined to the Chinatown districts established in many Californian towns, the largest in San Francisco holding 47,000 Chinese-Americans.

San Francisco Destroyed

Northern California's depression was further compounded by the calamitous **earthquake** which struck San Francisco in April 1906. The rupturing of gas and water mains led to a fire that burned across the city uncontrolled for three days, leaving 300 dead (officially), 250,000 homeless and the city in ruins.

The Rise of Southern California

The earthquake symbolized what was to be a permanent north to south shift in California's balance of power. With no fresh water supply and no natural harbour, **Los Angeles** seemed an unlikely spot to eventually become the USA's second-biggest city but money raised among its 5000 citizens was enough to bribe officials and bring a railroad to the town, rather than to the better situated San Diego, in 1885.

Los Angeles encouraged settlement by slashing rail fares from the east and offering large residential plots at knockdown prices. By the turn of the century, the city had 100,000 residents and was on a financial upswing thanks to the discovery of local oil deposits.

From the 1910s, a former Methodist temperance colony called **Hollywood** – separated by 8 miles (13km) of bean fields from Los Angeles proper – was being overrun by film-producers and their entourages. By the 1920s, film-making employed 100,000 people in Los Angeles and was among California's top 35 industries.

World War II and After

World War II brought a great influx of people into California and the state received 10% of all federal defence spending. San Francisco was the major embarkation point for the war in the Pacific, ship- and aircraft-building expanded all along the coast, and San Diego became – and continues to be – the base of the US Navy's Sixth Fleet.

At war's end, the aerospace industry continued to gather momentum, providing 60% of all new jobs between 1950 and 1963 and contributing greatly to the expansion of **Orange County**, immediately south of Los Angeles, which became the epitome of comfortable Southern Californian suburban living. The opening of **Disneyland**® in 1955, also in Orange County, helped fuel the myth of California as a place where dreams and reality were one and the same.

California also acquired a reputation as a place of dissent. The Beat Generation, the Free Speech Movement (the precursor to student-led anti-Vietnam War rallies), Hippies, Hells Angels and Black Panthers all made their first appearances in the state between the late 1950s and the end of the 1960s. From the late 1970s, the New Age movement – rebirthing, crystals, channelling and more – emerged and steadily spread around the globe, seeming perfectly suited to yet another enduring Californian image: that of spiritually adventurous and esoteric – or just plain odd – lifestyles.

From the early 1960s, San Francisco's **Haight-Ashbury** neighbourhood had been in the throes of a minor social revolution, aided by the still legal hallucinogenic drug, **LSD**, and music from local bands such as the Grateful Dead. As newspaper press coverage became increasingly sensational, many of the leading 'hippie' figures departed, but by the summer of 1967, Haight-Ashbury was filling with long-haired young people from all over the US: its population rising from 7000 to 75,000 in six months.

Below: *Motorcycle enthusiasts rendezvous in Los Angeles.*

Above: *The dome of the State Capitol, Sacramento.*
Below: *Downtown Los Angeles – man-made giants reach for the heavens.*

Farming has long been a major Californian occupation but when the 400-mile-long (644km) **San Joaquin Valley**, running through the centre of the state, was irrigated by the diverting of northern rivers during the 1930s, it became one of the world's most agriculturally productive regions. Together with the **Imperial Valley**, further south, the San Joaquin Valley enables California to grow more food than **90%** of the world's nations.

GOVERNMENT AND ECONOMY

California's chief executive is the governor, elected every four years by popular vote and eligible for unlimited re-election. The governor's duties include selecting a cabinet, making judicial appointments, and preparing the state budget for the approval of the **Senate**, the **Upper House** of the state's bicameral legislature.

The **Senate** consists of 40 members serving four-year terms, half of whom face re-election every two years. The **Lower House**, the **Assembly**, is composed of 80 members each elected every two years. Proposed new laws need the approval of both houses to be adopted. The governor has a veto but this may be overturned by a two-thirds majority in the Assembly and Senate.

In Washington DC, California is represented by 53 members of Congress and by two Senators. California is a major prize in the US presidential election, its large population bringing the winning candidate about 20% of the votes needed to attain office.

Aerospace, agriculture, entertainment (including film and TV), computer and electronic industries are among the major components in a diverse $1.6-trillion economy. Tourism, too, continues to be a key source of revenue, particularly in Los Angeles which has recovered spectacularly as a visitor destination since the 1992 riots. A sharp drop in federal defence spending through the 1990s caused the loss of many of the state's military-related

Where They Live

Los Angeles: 3.8 million
Los Angeles metropolitan area: 12.9 million
San Francisco: 740,000
Bay Area: 6.8 million
San Diego: 1.3 million

Left: *Grape harvesting in the Napa Valley.*

jobs. Further job losses resulted from companies moving to states offering lower taxes and cheaper labour.

In northern California, long-standing occupations such as **fishing** and **logging** have greatly declined due to reduced fish stocks and conservation initiatives. Since the gold rush, California has lost 90% of its redwoods and Douglas fir trees.

If California were a country, it would have one of the top ten economies in the world, though a surging economy can bring problems, such as those of San Francisco during the late-1990s dotcom boom when property prices rose so sharply as to drive the poor and the only-moderately wealthy out of the city.

THE PEOPLE

California is one of four American states without an ethnic majority. Anglo-Americans formed 70% of the state's population in 1980 but 20 years later the figure was 49%. Immigration from Latin America and a relatively high Latin American birthrate caused California's Latino population to grow by 70% in the 1980s. Through the same period, California's Asian population rose by 127%, due to the easing of restrictions on Chinese immigration and an influx of refugees from Southeast Asia. That this changing ethnicity has yet to be mirrored in political office is a constant source of tension.

CALIFORNIA COMMUNITIES

Early California held many short-lived communities with utopian aspirations. In 1878 actress **Helena Modjeska** arrived in **Anaheim** from Poland and helped found what locals dubbed the 'ill-fated artists' colony'.

Slightly more successful, peaking with 900 members in 1914, was **Llano del Rio**, a community founded by high-profile socialist **Job Harriman** on the edge of the **Mojave Desert**.

Dedicated to self-sufficiency (and unintentionally to ecological havoc), the **Kaweah Commonwealth** was a 400-strong Marxist logging colony, formed in 1885 in what is now **Sequoia National Park**.

Below: An everyday Chinatown street scene in San Francisco.

Since the gold rush, California has been growing at breakneck speed. The population doubled in the first two decades of the 20th century and the pace has seldom slowed since. The 26.5 million population of 1985 had swelled to 36 million 20 years later and is projected to reach 50 million by the year 2025. In 1995, only 45% of California residents were born in the state.

The rate of growth tends to conceal the fact that many Californians are actually leaving the state. Around 500,000 Anglo-Americans depart each year, often to the states of the Southwest and Pacific Northwest, and commonly cite concern over natural disasters, social and environmental problems, and the state's changing ethnicity, as reasons for doing so.

Latinos

Since 1945, Los Angeles has held the largest Mexican community outside **Mexico**, and through the 1950s California sought to fill the labour shortage on its farms by importing Mexican labour. Mexicans still provide the bulk of the manual work on Californian farms, though California's Latino population also includes people from all over South and Central America.

Expanding rapidly through the 1980s, Latino numbers increased to become 27% of California's adult population and more than half the child-age population: one in four Californians now speaks Spanish as a mother tongue. Two-thirds of the population is projected to be of Latino origin or descent by 2010. An inescapable fact for aspiring politicians is that once these youngsters reach voting age, political office may no longer be won – as it often is now – by appealing to the interests of the Anglo-American middle classes.

Asians

The **Chinese**, who have featured prominently in California since the gold rush, were victims of the 'Yellow Peril' hysteria of the late 1800s which forced them into Chinatown areas and caused the US government to stop further immigration from China. Immigration laws were only relaxed during the 1960s, a period which saw a great influx of Chinese, particularly from Hong Kong and Taiwan, into California. While the Chinatown areas of many Californian cities are very distinctive, many of their businesses are run by more recent arrivals from the war-stricken countries of Southeast Asia.

Through the 1970s and 1980s, 100,000 **Cambodian**, **Laotian** and **Vietnamese** refugees settled in California. Twenty years earlier, **Korean** communities were established in the wake of the Korean War. The Chinese, meanwhile, often became sufficiently wealthy and integrated into mainstream society to leave the confines of Chinatown for more comfortable suburbia. Three million people of Asian descent now live in California, a third of the USA's Asian-American total.

Above: *Serious volleyball at Santa Barbara.*

African-Americans

The USA's entry into World War II brought about a boom in new manufacturing industries in California and the need for labour encouraged African-Americans in the racially segregated states of the American Southeast to move west. By the 1950s, California's African-American numbers had risen nearly four fold and, by the early 1980s, almost two million lived in the state, forming nearly 8% of the population.

Recently, it seems that the African-Americans are as disillusioned with California as their Anglo-American counterparts, with significant numbers attracted by jobs in the rejuvenated economies of the Southeastern states.

INDIAN RESERVATIONS

The practice of settlers allocating unwanted land for Native American use (traditional native lands being usurped for farming) began in the pre-US period of the Californios. Surviving from this time are the **Morongo** reservation, near Palm Springs, and the **Pala** reservation near San Diego. The largest such area is the **Hoopa Valley** Reservation in Humboldt County, Northern California, covering 93,000 acres (38,000ha) and populated by around 2600 Hoopa people. About 35,000 of the state's 350,000 native population live on such lands.

Above: *Capturing the film crew in the early, heady days of Hollywood cinema.*

The Arts

California has been a meeting place of people and ideas since the gold rush and it should be no surprise that artistic pursuits are high on the state's list of achievements.

Film

Based in Los Angeles since the 1910s and quickly one of the state's major employers, the US film industry has done more than any other medium to show California to the world. Booming during the 1940s and 1950s but tempered since by the impact of television, **Hollywood** remains the place of big budgets and provides the ultimate challenge for every aspiring actor, screen writer and director.

Literature

From the 1930s in novels such as *The Big Sleep* and *Farewell, My Lovely*, **Raymond Chandler** captured a downbeat LA in a fiction style dubbed 'hard-boiled', a genre shared by former San Francisco private detective **Dashiell Hammett**, best known for creating *Sam Spade* and *The Maltese Falcon*. More realistic in approach, **John Steinbeck** chronicled California's ill-treated migrant workers, most famously with 1939's *The Grapes of Wrath*. More recently, **James Ellroy** has chronicled the sleazy side of LA policing, starting with *The Black Dahlia*. In San Francisco, **Amy Tan** portrayed several generations of Chinese-American lives in *The Joy Luck Club*.

Bernard Maybeck – born in New York but fresh from studying at the Ecole des Beaux Arts in Paris – settled in Berkeley in 1889. He became a familiar figure in his smock and beret and wielded considerable influence on Bay Area **architecture**. Though noted above all for his exuberant rustic homes (many of which succumbed to fire), a different approach led to Maybeck's most enduring creation, **San Francisco's Palace of Fine Arts** (see p. 40).

Music

The odes to girls and surfing of the **Beach Boys** defined California pop music from the early 1960s. By the end of the decade, however, San Francisco groups such as the **Grateful Dead** and **Jefferson Airplane** were fronting the hippie movement. As LA film companies diversified through the 1970s, they helped the city eclipse New York as the centre of the US music industry, a period which saw the international success of LA-based **Fleetwood Mac** and **The Eagles**. In the late 1980s, the harder sounds of **Guns & Roses** were the state's biggest success story. Through the 1990s, rap artists such as **Ice-T** and **Snoop Doggy Dog** found a global audience from the ghettos of South Central LA.

Architecture

When John Bakewell and Arthur Brown raised San Francisco City Hall in 1915, they not only gave California a **beaux-arts** masterpiece but also contributed to the state's rich diversity of architecture. Los Angeles saw the birth of the **California Bungalow**, originally a simple woodframed dwelling but soon sprouting porches, balconies and overhanging roofs. The same city gained much **Streamline Moderne Art Deco** and acquired a féted example of the **International Style** with Richard Neutra's 1929 **Lovell House**, 4616 Dundee Drive.

Now seen everywhere from shopping malls to motels, the red roofs, belltowers and courtyards of the **Mission Style**, a form of Mediterranean Revival derived from the state's Spanish missions, became fashionable in the 1920s as Southern California marketed itself as the American Mediterranean.

Recent Californian architecture includes the **Los Angeles Museum of Contemporary Art**, Arata Isozaki's fusing of Asian and American themes in sandstone, and Frank Gehry's sublimely curved Disney Concert Hall, also in Los Angeles.

Even though much of his best work has been overseas – such as **Basle's Vitra Centre** and Bilbao's extraordinary **Guggenheim Museum** – one of the most influential and respected of California's contemporary architects is Frank Gehry. Among his most celebrated works are his own Los Angeles house, a pink 1920s structure revamped by the owner with a generous application of industrial materials (the neighbour-enraging residence stands at 1002, 22nd Street, Santa Monica) and Los Angeles' Disney Concert Hall, completed in 2004.

Below: *Shimmering San Francisco at night, seen through the struts of the Golden Gate Bridge.*

Sport and Recreation

California has its share of couch potatoes but a much more common sight are the fit and active physiques which indicate a passion for outdoor pursuits. For visitors, too, the state offers activities to suit all tastes in all seasons.

Surfing might seem the quintessential Californian sport though it began in Hawaii and surged in popularity in California only after the invention of the lightweight surfboard in the 1950s. Much of the Southern Californian coast is excellent surfing territory; other noted areas are around Santa Barbara and Santa Cruz.

Ski resorts around Lake Tahoe, and in Mammoth Lakes and Bishop in the Eastern Sierra, do a roaring trade through the snowy season, usually September to April, and are exceptionally crowded at weekends. Usually less busy are the more northerly ski runs around Mount Shasta in the Cascade Mountains.

The **mountain bike**, devised for racing on the hills north of San Francisco, is ideal for tackling the steep terrain common across California. In summer, ski-runs at Mammoth Lakes are converted into a huge mountain biking track. Even for the less energetic, **cycling** can bring much gentle and happy touring; even sections of car-dominated Los Angeles have marked cycle routes. Bike rental outlets are numerous.

Below: *Golf in the desert: a course at Palm Springs overlooked by the San Jacinto mountains.*

Laced with **hiking trails** which can be explored over a few hours or a few weeks, California's back-country, particularly through the Sierra Nevada and above Big Sur, reveals fabulous scenery. Such trails are not to be undertaken lightly, however. Hikers should always be fully prepared and equipped, heed the advice of park rangers, and be protective of the environment. Rental equipment and information can be found at the major trail heads.

Food and Drink

Californian eating spans everything from the delectable morsels of **California Cuisine** to the filling fare of the great all-American **coffee shop**, all benefiting from the state's bumper agricultural crop and the widespread knowledge that healthy eating is good eating. The competition to satiate your appetite – San Francisco alone has 4000 restaurants – means prices are seldom excessive and only the most elaborate dinner in a luxurious setting will seriously dent your budget.

Breakfast is best eaten in a local **diner** or coffee shop. Breakfasts can conform to the US high-cholesterol standard: a choice of omelettes or eggs fried to order, with or without **hash browns** (grated fried potato), toast (wholewheat, rye, or white), ham, bacon and sausages. California's **omelettes** commonly include three separate fillings, one of which is usually cheese – Swiss, Cheddar, American or the Californian-made **Monterey Jack**. Another omelette option is the 'Mexican', packed with vegetables with a fiery coating of chilli sauce. Many establishments also carry a range of fruit and cereals to serve separately or with the traditional breakfast fare.

Above: *Skiers head for the slopes above Lake Tahoe.*

White-Water Rafting

During early summer, the melting snows on the peaks of California's mountains cause river levels to rise and conditions become perfect for white-water rafting. Trips are organized by a number of companies, with the densest concentration near **Yosemite National Park**. For details, contact the **Tuolumne County Visitors Center**; tel: toll free 1-800 446-1333.

For **lunch**, most diners and coffee shops offer an inexpensive variety of sandwiches (entire meals between slices of bread) and some have tasty homemade soups served by the cup (for a snack) or bowl (for a meal). In slightly smarter establishments, a Californian salad is a wise choice as a main dish, typically featuring a deep bed of lettuce heaped with cheese, strawberries, grapes, avocado, orange slices, and much more, depending on what is in season.

For many Californians, going out for **dinner** is a vital part of everyday life and local newspaper restaurant reviews are avidly read. Predictably, the more you spend the better the meal and the surroundings are likely to be, though the impact of 1970s **Californian Cuisine** – small, perfectly prepared and artistically arranged meals based on the freshest local ingredients and the chef's blending of recipes from near and far – has filtered down into the medium-priced eateries. The best bet in many quality restaurants is the nightly special, which will make the most of seasonal fare and the chef's inspiration.

Many ethnic restaurants are extremely good value and seafood, too, is prevalent. Look out for the creamy **Dungeness crab** during its mid-November to June season. Swordfish, snapper, squid and baby octopus are also common menu components.

Approximately 90% of the **wine** consumed in the USA originates in California.

When a Chardonnay from California's **Napa Valley** won a prestigious Parisian tasting in 1976, the scene was set for the international rise of the state's wine industry, concentrated in the **Napa** and **Sonoma** valleys.

Most bar and restaurants will have a decent stock of Californian wines though the place to learn more is, obviously, a winery; most offer free tours and tastings. California's consistent climate causes vintages to have little meaning and, unlike in Europe, Californian wines are made from – and named for – a single grape type.

Many Californians stick to the dependable dry, white **Chardonnay** though one curiosity worth trying is **Zinfandel**, available as a white wine despite the Zinfandel grape – a type unknown outside the USA – being red. American **beers** such as Budweiser, Coors, and Miller, lack strength and flavour compared to their European counterparts, but California has enjoyed a micro-brewery revolution with a growing number of dedicated beer makers producing notable beers in small breweries, usually part of a bar or restaurant. Also available are imported beers, among them Heineken, Dos Equis and Tecate.

Spirits can only be served in bars and fully-licensed restaurants, which tend to be the more expensive establishments. **Cocktails** are common; any type you order is unlikely to perplex a properly trained bartender, who is also likely to suggest a few exotic local versions.

Vietnamese and **Cambodian** are just two of the ethnic eating choices that reflect the state's most recent immigrant groups. Already well established are **Chinese** (with regional Chinese cuisines strongly represented), **Thai**, **Italian**, **Japanese**. Slightly less common are **Greek**, **Indian** and **Middle Eastern** restaurants. **Mexican** is by far the most prevalent of the Central American cuisines, though Mexican restaurants usually make much more use of fruit and vegetables than is the case in Mexico itself.

Opposite: *Sunny weather and excellent cuisine are synonymous with the Californian lifestyle.*
Left: *Fresh seafood without pretensions.*

2
San Francisco and the Bay Area

With water on three sides and green hills in the distance, **San Francisco** sits at the tip of a peninsula enjoying the most enviable natural setting imaginable. Even the fog, which regularly dulls the city's mornings, heightens the natural drama by wrapping a white blanket around the **Golden Gate Bridge** and the taller buildings until the sun burns through and bathes the city in light. Likewise, the 40 hills across which the city spreads may sap the leg muscles but provide a view supreme from almost every corner.

Since the mid-19th-century gold rush boosted its population from 500 to 25,000 in two years and helped make it the **ninth-largest city** in the US by the turn of the 20th century, San Francisco has a been place of promise and opportunity. Openness to new ideas and unconventional lifestyles saw the city give birth to beatniks and hippies, and enabled gay men and lesbians to be integrated into the city's political machine. Through the 1990s, San Francisco and nearby Silicon Valley were at the forefront of the dot-com boom, and the subsequent bust, that had great impact on the area.

Seeing San Francisco is enjoyable and easy. Many neighbourhoods and sights can be reached and toured on foot and the whole city – 7 miles (11km) from bay to ocean – can be crossed on a 20-minute bus ride. Many 'San Franciscans' actually live outside the city in the **Bay Area**, which encompasses **Berkeley**, **Oakland** and **Marin County**, and other parts of the peninsula south of San Francisco, all of which warrant a visit.

DON'T MISS

*** North Beach: old Italian neighbourhood packed with cafés, bistros and beatniks.
*** Chinatown: biggest Asian community outside Asia.
*** Alcatraz Island: remains of an infamous prison.
*** Golden Gate Bridge: modern engineering as art.
** Golden Gate Park: among the world's largest urban parks.
** Yerba Buena Gardens: home to the Museum of Modern Art and more.

Opposite: *San Francisco and the landmark Golden Gate Bridge.*

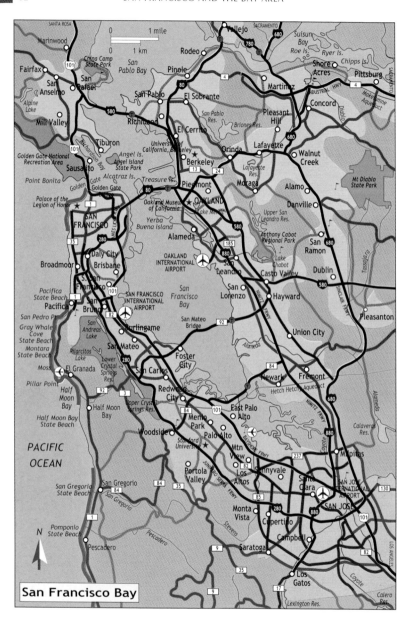

San Francisco Bay

SAN FRANCISCO NEIGHBOURHOODS

San Francisco divides into many tightly grouped neighbourhoods, sometimes only a few strides apart but – from the temples of **Chinatown** to the neo-hippies of **Haight-Ashbury** – each infused with a distinctive style and character. Get to know its neighbourhoods and you get to know San Francisco.

Financial District ★

The commercial lifeblood of the city, the Financial District's banks and insurance companies fill glass-and-steel high-rises clustered around the eastern end of Market Street. Among them is the **Transamerica Pyramid**, 600 Montgomery Street, a symbol of the city since its 1972 completion, and the towering 555 California Street, formerly known as the Bank of America Building. Among the few brick buildings, seek out the 1903 **Merchants' Exchange Building**, 465 California Street, a reminder of San Francisco's maritime trading heyday with wonderful nautically themed frescoes on the ground floor (currently unoccupied, but glimpse the murals through the locked doors). Also visit the **Pacific Stock Exchange**, 301 Pine Street, a 1930s re-working of a 1915 building and fronted by an imposing pair of stone sculptures.

Chinatown ★★★

Packed with Asian restaurants (Vietnamese and Cambodian eateries among the longer-established Chinese) and decorated by dragon-tail entwined lampposts and pagoda-style buildings such as the 1909 **Bank of Canton**, 743 Washington Street, Chinatown fills just 24 blocks but holds the biggest Asian community outside of Asia. Busy Grant Avenue is lined by enjoyable though clearly tourist-aimed shops; detour along Waverly Place and the reward is the **Tien How Temple**, number 125, dating from 1852 and the oldest of Chinatown's temples. Through informative exhibitions, the **Chinese Historical Society of America**, 965 Clay Street, illuminates the story of Chinese immigration to California.

Below: *A nostalgic reminder of early San Francisco when trams were the only form of public transport.*

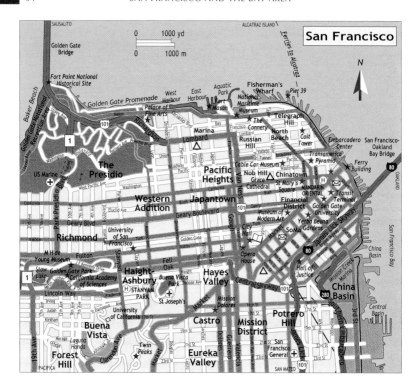

North Beach ★★★

Settled by Italians from the 1890s, North Beach began San Francisco's lasting affection for cafés, cappuccino and Italian food. In the 1950s, the **City Lights** bookstore opened at 247 Columbus Avenue and published the first major work by poet Allen Ginsberg, the precursor to a North Beach invasion of what a city newspaper columnist dubbed 'beatniks'.

North Beach's Italian landmarks include the imposing twin-spired **Church of Sts Peter and Paul**, overlooking Washington Square, and Caffé Trieste, 601 Vellejo Street, with excellent snacks and amateur opera performances on Saturday afternoons. **Caffé Trieste** was a favourite beatnik rendezvous, as was the bar **Vesuvio**, 255 Columbus Avenue, still in business, almost next door to the similarly still-thriving City Lights.

THE CASTRO

San Francisco holds the largest gay community in the world and many of the city's gays reside in the Castro, between Haight-Ashbury and the Mission District. Residents of the area have higher-than-average incomes, and the Castro sports many very well-looked-after Victorian homes. The 1923 **Castro Theater**, 429 Castro Street, is a local landmark.

Nob Hill ★★

Nob Hill has been San Francisco's most exclusive address since the Big Four (*see* p. 17) built mansions on it in the 1880s. All the mansions, bar one (now housing the Pacific Union Club, facing California Street), were destroyed in the 1906 fire. In their place are many high-rise apartment blocks, several luxury hotels, the compact and relaxing **Huntington Park**, and the Episcopalian **Grace Cathedral**, 1051 Taylor Street, completed in 1964 and partly modelled on Paris's Notre Dame.

Above: *Stately Victorian homes with a Financial District backdrop.*

Russian Hill ★★

Today, doctors, dentists and Financial District high flyers are the people able to afford Russian Hill's property prices, though in the 1890s the neighbourhood was the home of San Francisco bohemia. Its denizens included architect Willis Polk (several of his shingle-walled structures remain) and literary luminaries such as Ina Coolbrith. In 1919, Coolbrith became California's first poet laureate and is remembered by the lush park which bears her name at the junction of Vellejo and Taylor streets.

Just to the north of the park, slender **Macandray Lane** epitomizes all that is good about Russian Hill: well-maintained cottages shaded by trees and wonderful views over the city. However, few visitors stumble across Macandray Lane, although most do make a bee-line for the much-photographed section of **Lombard Street** between **Hyde** and **Leavenworth** streets, where the very steep gradient is made driveable by a series of corkscrew bends framed by immaculate gardens.

Pacific Heights ★

To get the measure of Pacific Heights, browse the chic boutiques and fancy restaurants that line **Union Street** (between Webster Street and Van Ness Avenue), the main shopping and socializing strip of the city's most

Above: *The marina, Fisherman's Wharf.*

affluent residential neighbourhood. Climbing Octavio Street to Lafayette Park reveals the 42-room **Spreckels Mansion**, the pick of Pacific Heights' countless impressive homes. Raised in fetching beaux-arts style, it was built to please the French-born wife of sugar mogul Adolph Spreckels in 1912.

Haight-Ashbury ★★

Haight-Ashbury became the centre of the world's hippie movement in the late 1960s but the sheer volume of young people arriving in the district caused idealistic beginnings to be overtaken by crime and hard-drug use. By the 1980s, however, Haight-Ashbury was in the throes of gentrification with many of its roomy and ornate Victorian homes – such as 301 Lyon Street and the former residence of rock band, the **Grateful Dead**, at 710 Ashbury Street – being restored. Nonetheless, the used-record and book shops, tie-dyed T-shirt stalls, sidewalk skateboarders and countless posters for poetry and music events scattered along **Haight Street**, all attest to the neighbourhood's continuing counter-cultural leanings.

Mission District ★

Though gaining an influx of affluent Anglos during the dot-com boom, the Mission District still holds a large Latino population. The commercial centre is around the junction of 24th and Mission streets but continue to **Balmy Alley** to view the best of the district's many large and colourful murals. The structure that gives the area its name is the oldest in San Francisco: **Mission Dolores**, 320 Dolores Street (open daily 09:00–16:00), founded by the Spanish in 1776 and the sixth of California's 21 missions. These days, the modern Basilica next door fulfils local religious needs but the mission's tiny chapel, small museum and very large cemetery, all evoke San Francisco's Spanish past.

PLACES OF INTEREST
From the engineering miracle of the **Golden Gate Bridge** to the notorious former prison of **Alcatraz**, the sights of San Francisco are seldom run of the mill. Nonetheless, even arch traditionalists in search of quality art and history collections are in for a treat.

Alcatraz Island ★★★
Between 1934 and 1963, Alcatraz Island, reached by a short ferry ride from **Fisherman's Wharf**, was the USA's highest security prison, surrounded by treacherous waters. Its inmates were deprived of newspapers, radio and TV, and only one in five ever received a visitor during an average period of incarceration lasting 10 years. The severity of the regime, coupled with the high costs of running an island prison, led to the prison's closure in 1963; it opened to the public nine years later.

The excellent self-guided tours feature a gripping commentary (on rented audio cassette and player) from former guards and inmates, and lead visitors through the cell blocks, canteen, hospital, and the exercise yard, where prisoners were tormented by the sights and sounds of San Francisco, less than 2 miles (3km) away.

Golden Gate Bridge ★★★
Completed in 1937, Golden Gate Bridge instantly became an emblem of San Francisco and continues to be a vital communications artery between the city and **Marin County**, with about 42 million vehicle crossings annually. For the fullest sense of the structure's size, cross its 2 mile-span (3km) on foot, peering down at the treacherous waters of the Golden Gate 220ft (67m) below.

ASIAN ART MUSEUM

Near the junction of Larkin and McAllister streets in Civic Center, the Asian Art Museum holds treasures spanning 6000 years drawn from Asia's religions, countries and cultures. The Chinese galleries are a feast of porcelains, jades and calligraphy from several dynasties. Elsewhere are marvellous Japanese Edo-period screen paintings, a wonderful stash of 18th- and 19th-century netsuke, and Hindu, Buddhist and Jain sculptures dominating the Indian galleries.

Below: *Alcatraz Island, seen from Hyde Street.*

Above: *Golden Gate Park's Conservatory of Flowers.*

SoMa

Named as an abbreviation of its 'South of Market Street' location, SoMa was the city's industrial sector until the 1970s, when changing transport patterns led to many of its warehouses being abandoned. By the 1980s, artists and cutting-edge nightclubs were making use of the spacious structures, and were steadily followed (and ousted as rents rose) by trendy media and design companies in search of office space. The area's biggest boost has been **Yerba Buena Gardens**.

Golden Gate Park ★★★

A verdant swathe between Haight-Ashbury and the Pacific Ocean, Golden Gate Park fills 1018 acres (412ha) and easily finds room for a golf course, a polo field, a herd of buffalo, riding stables, and several lakes.

Also in the park, grouped in close proximity near the eastern entrance, are two of San Francisco's biggest visitor attractions. At the **MH de Young Museum** a major stash of American arts and crafts spans 17th-century New England interiors, Shaker furniture, paintings by Albert Bierstadt, sculpture by Frederic Remington, and contemporary works from Bay Area artists. This and much more is contained within the creatively designed space that seeks to fuse the building into the natural landscape of the park. Open Tuesday–Sunday 09:30–17:15.

A better stop for children is the stupendously designed **California Academy of Sciences** (due to re-open here in late 2008; until then located in SoMa at 875 Howard Street), with the state-of-the-art Steinhart Aquarium packed with creatures of the mysterious deep, and many other imaginitive exhibits intended to explain and excite interest in the natural world. Open daily 10:00–17:00.

Green-fingered park visitors might skip the museums in favour of the **Conservatory of Flowers**, the exquisitely laid out **Japanese Tea Garden**, and the **Strybing Arboretum and Botanical Gardens**, with its collection of 6000 plant types filling 70 acres (28ha).

Yerba Buena Gardens ★★★

The rejuvenation of SoMa transformed a 12-block segment directly south of Mission Street into the city's artistic and cultural heart. The area's major component is the **San Francisco Museum of Modern Art**, 151 Third Street, an unmistakeable black-and-white striped cylinder rising from its roof to bring light streaming into the interior. Open Tuesday–Sunday 11:00–18:00; Thursday 11:00–21:00. Open at 10:00 during summer.

The main galleries feature 20th-century European greats – **Picasso**, **Braque**, **Matisse**, **Klee**, **Ernst**, **Dali** and many more – with a good helping of American abstract expressionists, such as **Pollock**, **De Kooning** and **Newman**. Recent acquisitions have greatly increased the museum's stock of valuable work by contemporary, and often controversial, figures, among them **Jeff Koons** and **Cindy Sherman**. Be sure to visit the galleries devoted to Californian art and find time to peruse the selections spanning the career of painter, **Richard Diebenkorn**. The architecture and design rooms hold much to intrigue, while the fourth floor focuses on interactive and computer art, as well as showing TV, video and film work. Among the contributors to the museum's rich collection of US and European photography is San Francisco-born Ansel Adams, noted for his depictions of landscapes. Other worthwhile stops close by include the California Historical Society (678 Mission Street), the Museum of Arts and Crafts (52 Yerba Buena Lane), the Cartoon Art Museum (655 Mission Street) and the Mexican Museum (due to open at 701 Mission Street).

Above: *Revitalizing the SoMa district, Yerba Buena Gardens is San Francisco's new arts and culture complex; the truncated cylinder of the Museum of Modern Art stands out.*

California Palace of the Legion of Honor ★★

On a dramatic site above the Golden Gate in Lincoln Park, is the California Palace of the Legion of Honor. Modelled on its namesake in Paris, it houses San Francisco's major trove of pre-20th-century European art. The collections stemmed from the friendship of Alma Spreckels, wife of wealthy San Franciscan Adolph Spreckels, with sculptor **Auguste Rodin**. The collection's 400 Rodin sculptures include a *Thinker* from the original cast, which greets visitors as they approach the entrance. Open Tuesday–Sunday 10:00–16:45.

Except for the gallery devoted to Rodin, the exhibits are arranged chronologically, enabling visitors to walk through some 700 years of artistic endeavour and feast

BERKELEY CAMPUS TOURS

Drawing a mixture of tourists and would-be undergraduates with their parents in tow, free student-led tours of the Berkeley campus depart at 10:00 on weekdays from the Visitors' Center, near the junction of Oxford Street and University Avenue. On Saturday and Sunday at 10:00 and 13:00 respectively, tours depart from Sather Tower.

their eyes on everything from medieval tapestries to **Georges Seurat's** shimmering **Eiffel Tower** of 1890. As you leave, follow the path from the car park to the **Holocaust Sculpture**, **George Segal's** evocative reminder of Nazi atrocities during World War II.

Palace of Fine Arts ★★

Designed by architect Bernard Maybeck for the 1915 Panama-Pacific Exposition, which celebrated the opening of the **Panama Canal** and symbolized San Francisco's recovery from the 1906 earthquake, the Palace of Fine Arts, west end of Lyon Street, was intended to resemble a Roman ruin. Its 132ft-high (40m), domed rotunda is flanked with a fragmented colonnade, and each group of columns is topped by weeping maidens and funeral urns. As the other Expo buildings were demolished, the Palace of Fine Arts survived, becoming a much-loved city landmark.

EXCURSIONS

San Francisco is a good base for day-trip excursions. To the east, **Berkeley** and **Oakland** are respectively the sites of a world-renowned university and a tremendous museum devoted to California. North, across the bay in **Marin County**, lie the hillside villages of **Sausalito** and **Tiburon**. Venturing south into the San Francisco peninsula, the only detour for which a car is essential, you reach the science-orientated **Stanford University** and the 'Silicon Valley' of San Jose.

Below: *Bernard Maybeck's intentional ruin: the Palace of Fine Arts.*

Berkeley ★★

The suburb of Berkeley is dominated by the 30,000 students of the **University of California** at Berkeley (UCB). Its 100-acre (41ha) campus is a few minutes walk north of the town's **BART** station (underground system) and 20 minutes from San Francisco.

The **University Art Museum** (open Wednesday–Sunday 11:00–17:00; Thursday 11:00–19:00) and the **Phoebe Hearst Museum of Anthropology** (open Wednesday–Friday 10:00–16:30; weekends 12:00–

16:00) merit a short visit. Time is better spent, though, wandering around the campus admiring the work of John Galen Howard, the architect charged with overseeing its construction in the early 1900s. Howard's contributions include **Sather Tower**, the centrally sited belltower, the nearby **Sather Gate**, and the beaux-arts **Hearst School of Mining**, in the campus's northeast corner.

The student-led Free Speech Movement began at UCB in 1964 and was the stimulus to the anti-Vietnam War protests which swept across the USA in the 1960s and early 1970s. UCB students are generally less politically active nowadays but a lunchtime stroll along **Sproul Plaza** finds sticker-plastered stalls promoting countless causes from around the world.

Oakland ★★

Reached from Berkeley by **BART** (underground system) or directly from San Francisco by ferry, the blue-collar city of Oakland holds the **Oakland Museum of California**, 1000 Oak Street, which will greatly improve your knowledge of the whys and wherefores of the Golden State. Open Wednesday–Saturday 10:00–17:00; Sunday 12:00–17:00.

At ground level, the **Hall of Ecology and Aquatic California Gallery** examines the diversity of natural California but, for all but the most devoted naturalist, the best part of the museum is the second-floor **Cowell Hall of History**. Be they the pioneer-period wagons or wacky 1950s souvenirs of Disneyland®, the exhibits are many and are very accessibly arranged. Individual items are not labelled but their details are held on user-friendly computers, which also offer the chance to explore particular historical avenues more thoroughly.

On the top floor, the collection of Californian art is arranged to show the swift progress of the state's artistic achievements, from rough sketches of gold-rush scenes to the multimedia work of contemporary artists.

Below: *An older section of the University of California at Berkeley.*

Above: *Relaxation on the bay – Sausalito.*

A short walk north of the museum along Oak Street leads to **Lake Merritt**, the world's largest saltwater lagoon, and the 1876 **Camron Stanford House**, 1418 Lakeside Drive. The restored house reveals something of early Oakland life while an introductory film tells the full story of Oakland, a community long tired of playing second-fiddle to San Francisco. Open Wednesdays 11:00–16:00; Sundays 13:00–17:00.

Marin County ★★

The rugged, undeveloped hills of Marin County provide a great contrast to San Francisco. Nestled at their foot are the picturesque villages of Sausalito and Tiburon, served by ferries from Fisherman's Wharf. In summer, ferries continue to Angel Island State Park, an uninhabited fist of greenery rising from San Francisco Bay.

Sausalito ★★

Though besieged by day trippers and holding a few too many gift shops, Sausalito has an appealing setting and photogenic views of San Francisco from any high point.

Escape the crowds by walking north along **Bayside**, passing colourful houseboats and, after 1 mile (1.6km), reaching the **Bay Model**, 2100 Bridgeway. Built by the **US Army Corp of Engineers**, the intriguing model is the size of an American football pitch and produces accurate replication of the tides and currents of San Francisco Bay. Open Tuesday–Saturday 09:00–16:00.

Tiburon ★

Tiburon, at the tip of a narrow peninsula, is slightly less busy than Sausalito. Weekend arrivals are greeted by the brightly painted shops of Main Street – some (known as **Ark Row**) are actually 19th-century houseboats pulled permanently ashore.

MUIR WOODS

Should you not be travelling further north along the coast, take the opportunity to see the **redwood trees** of Marin County's Muir Woods National Monument. This redwood grove may not hold the tallest examples in the state but does give a good idea of what the mighty trees are all about. Muir Woods is accessible on guided tours from San Francisco, by car, or by a lengthy cycle ride from Sausalito.

Angel Island State Park ★★

The largest island in San Francisco Bay, Angel Island State Park is ideal for hiking, cycling or simply munching a picnic while enjoying a splendid view of San Francisco. Trails pass small beaches and the remnants of abandoned military installations before reaching the island's 781ft (238m) summit.

The Peninsula and San José ★

Several points of note dot the otherwise uniformly suburban 44 miles (71km) between San Francisco and San José. At Palo Alto, **Stanford University**, among the world's leading private educational institutions, was founded in 1891 by railroad baron Leland Stanford in memory of his son. **Hoover Tower** gives a bird's eye view across the campus, its older sections attractively designed in Romanesque style.

Since 1967, the university's **Stanford Linear Accelerator** has been firing protons along a 2-mile (3km) course. Anyone who does not have a clue what this means is advised to take the elucidating two-hour tour (tel: (650) 926-4931) explaining the accelerator's importance and its mysterious powers.

Santa Clara Valley was at the forefront of the personal computer revolution of the 1980s, earning the nickname 'Silicon Valley' and enabling **San José** to become the state's fastest-growing city. San José's modernistic centre The Tech Museum of Innovation, 201 S Market Street (open Tuesday–Sunday 10:00–17:00), celebrates pioneering technology in all forms.

Elsewhere, construction of the **Winchester Mystery House**, 525 S Winchester Boulevard, continued for 38 years because owner Sarah Winchester, heir to the family firearm fortunes, believed that she would die if building ever stopped. Consequently, the house acquired 160 rooms, 2000 doors and 10,000 windows. Open daily 09:00–16:00 or 19:00. The esoteric **Rosicrucian Foundation** built their international base at 1342 Naglee Avenue. In its **Rosicrucian Egyptian Museum** are displayed a formidable stash of antiquities from Egypt, Assyria and Babylon. Open Monday–Friday 10:00–17:00; weekends 11:00–18:00.

ENVIRONMENTAL AWARENESS

Just east of San Mateo, roughly half way between San Francisco and Palo Alto, the **Coyote Point Museum** informs on the threatened ecosystems of San Francisco Bay with revealing displays and hands-on exhibits. Increasing industrial and residential use of the land around the bay, and the lessening of fresh water reaching it due to the damming of its inland feeder rivers, are both having a detrimental effect on the bay's ability to sustain a rich assortment of wildlife.

San Francisco at a Glance

Though fog is common in the early morning and evening, San Francisco enjoys a mild year-round climate and can be visited at any time. The fog is generally at its worst during the summer, leaving **September** and **October** as the sunniest and most pleasant months. Temperatures seldom drop to uncomfortable depths during winter, although January brings San Francisco's heaviest rainfall.

San Francisco is a major international and domestic air hub with strong links across the state. Northern California's freeways and highways provide direct access to the city via the Golden Gate or Bay bridges. San Francisco is a two-hour **drive** from Sacramento or Santa Cruz, and eight hours from Los Angeles. Direct Greyhound **buses** are frequent from Los Angeles and Sacramento; much less so from other parts of California. Amtrak **trains** stop on the east side of the bay at Emeryville, from where free **coaches** carry passengers into the city.

San Francisco is easy to travel around and a car is not required. Neighbourhoods can be safely explored on **foot** and, where distances are greater, a comprehensive **bus** network is inexpensive and simple to use.

BART (underground system) is an efficient alternative to buses across distances, notably to Berkeley and Oakland; **ferries** link the city with Marin County and Oakland.

LUXURY
Mandarin Oriental, 222 Sansome Street, tel: (415) 276-9888, fax: 986-0289. Occupying the top section of a 48-storey Financial District tower and offering everything, plus stunning views.
Ritz-Carlton, 600 Stockton Street, tel: (415) 296-7465, fax: (415) 364-3455. Highly skilled in the art of pampering.
Westin St Francis, 335 Powell Street, tel: (415) 397-7000, fax: (415) 774-0125. A San Francisco landmark since 1904, history and tradition are the main reasons for staying here; service is first rate.

MID-RANGE
The Red Victorian, 1665 Haight Street, tel: (415) 864-1978, fax: (415) 863-3293. In mood and décor, perfectly mixing the spirit of 1960s with 1990s New Age California.
Stanyan Park Hotel, 750 Stanyan Street, tel: (415) 751-1000, fax: (415) 668-5454. An Edwardian hotel, convenient for exploring Haight-Ashbury.
Washington Square Inn, 1660 Stockton Street, tel: (415) 981-4220, fax: (415) 397-7242. Simple, no frills but tastefully furnished rooms.

BUDGET
Grant Plaza, 465 Grant Avenue, tel: (415) 434-3883, fax (415) 434-3886. Compact Chinatown hotel, small rooms but entirely adequate.
San Francisco Hostelling International, Building 240, Fort Mason Center, tel: (415) 771-7277, fax: (415) 771-1468. The biggest youth hostel in the USA but also the one with the most spectacular setting, beside the Golden Gate. Excellent value for money.
San Remo Hotel, 2237 Mason Street, tel: (415) 776-8688, fax: (415) 776-2811. Renovated 1906 Italianate villa; rooms lack private bathrooms but have heaps of atmosphere.

LUXURY
Aqua, 252 California Street, tel: (415) 956-9662, fax: (415) 956-5229. Fresh seafood served in delicate, artful portions to a chic crowd.
Dining room at the Ritz-Carlton, 600 Stockton Street, tel: (415) 773-6168, fax: (415) 291-0147. Multiple award-winning spot for special-occasion dining.
Green's, Building A, Fort Mason Center, tel: (415) 771-6222. Using produce grown on an organic farm, Green's serves expensive but ultra-healthy and charmingly prepared vegetarian meals.
Tommy Toy's, 655 Montgomery Street, tel: (415) 397-4888, fax: (415) 397-0469

For many years the city's most celebrated Chinese restaurant, mixing ideas from Asian and French cuisine.

MID-RANGE

Brandy Ho's, 450 Broadway, tel: (415) 788-7527. A local legend for delicious and spicy Hunan cuisine in an unpretentious setting.

John's Grill, 63 Ellis Street, tel: (415) 986-0069. The food is good quality all-American steak and seafood fare but the reason to pay a call is the Dashiell Hammett connection: the writer's fictional sleuth, Sam Spade, regularly dined here and is remembered by memorabilia in the upstairs dining room.

The Stinking Rose, 325 Columbus Avenue, tel: (415) 781-7673, fax: (415) 781-2833. Serves a range of Italian dishes and seasons absolutely all of them with garlic.

Tomasso's, 1042 Kearny Street, tel: (415) 398-9696. Popular for Italian fare in North Beach.

BUDGET

Dottie's True Blue Café, 522 Jones Street, tel: (415) 885-2767. A modern rendition of the traditional American coffee shop, with friendly service, low prices and many health-conscious options.

Eagle Café, Pier 39, Fisherman's Wharf, tel: (415) 433-3689. Serving breakfast, lunch and dinner since 1928; a welcome find among the area's many tourist-aimed eateries.

House of Nanking, 919 Kearny Street, tel: (415) 421-1429. Northern regional Chinese cuisine served at prices low enough to make the wait worthwhile.

Pho Hao, Ground Level, Three Embarcadero Center, tel: (415) 399-9099. Global chain specializing in Vietnamese noodle-soup dishes.

Yank Sing, 101 Spear Street, tel: (415) 957-9300, fax: (415) 957-9899. Dim sum, the Chinese lunchtime speciality of small dishes ordered from passing trolleys. This outlet is slightly pricier than some but worth the visit as it is the best.

SHOPPING

The main streets of San Francisco's diverse neighbourhoods often reward intrepid shoppers: in particular, Chinatown's Grant Avenue, Haight-Ashbury's Haight Street, and Pacific Heights' Union Street are worth at least an hour's window browsing. For general shopping, renowned department stores such as **Saks Fifth Avenue**, **Macy's** and **Neiman Marcus** ring Union Square.

TOURS AND EXCURSIONS

Free walking tours are operated daily in different parts of the city by **City Guides**, tel: (415) 557-4266, www.sfcityguides.org Recommended paid walking tours which are reasonably priced are **Wok Wiz**, tel: (650) 355-9657, www.wokwiz.com covering Chinatown, and **Cruisin' the Castro**, tel: (415) 255-1821, www.crusinthecastro.com examining San Francisco's gay and lesbian landmarks and alternative lifestyles. Boat tours on San Francisco Bay are offered by the **Red & White Fleet**, tel: (415) 901-5254, www.redandwhite.com and the **Blue & Gold Fleet**, tel: (415) 705-8200, www.blueandgoldfleet.com Aerial Tours of the city and bay: **San Francisco Helicopter Tours and Charter**, tel: toll free 1-800 400-2404, www.sfhelicopter tours.com

USEFUL CONTACTS

San Francisco Visitor Information Center, Hallidie Plaza, tel: (415) 391-2000, www.sfcvb.org

SAN FRANCISCO	J	F	M	A	M	J	J	A	S	O	N	D
AVERAGE TEMP. °C	9	10	11	13	14	16	16	17	17	15	12	10
AVERAGE TEMP. °F	48	50	52	55	57	61	61	63	63	59	54	50
DAYS OF RAINFALL	11	11	10	6	4	2	0	0	2	4	7	10
RAINFALL mm	127	76	76	51	25	12	0	0	12	25	76	102
RAINFALL in	5	3	3	2	1	0.4	0	0	0.4	1	3	4

3
Northern California and the Wine Country

With the exception of the much-visited Wine Country, the third of California that lies north of San Francisco is a total mystery – to many Californians as well as to travellers. Cloaked in fog, raining for nine months of the year and with few towns of appreciable size scattered across its gaping tracts of undeveloped land, the north is California as few people imagine it: wet, cold and sparsely populated.

The 380 miles (611km) of coast between the **Bay Area** and the **Oregon** border is dotted with inlet-hugging villages, windswept beaches, and bluffs that loom above an ocean too chilly and treacherous for anyone to even think about swimming. Yet the extreme conditions are the appeal: the sweeping scale of nature's handiwork is what excites. Much the same applies to the inland north, where long drives separate points of interest and friendly small towns where everybody knows everybody else. But, again, the landscapes are to be treasured: **snowcapped mountains** and **vast forests** holding damp, dark groves of towering redwood trees. Press deeper, into the **volcanic lands** of the state's northeastern extremity, and the outlook becomes wilder still.

The **Wine Country** is a different story. Amid gentle, rolling countryside, the short **Napa** and **Sonoma** valleys each hold a string of appealing small towns and an entirely disproportionate number of wineries. Add to this a generous endowment of spa resorts and the Wine Country becomes a place ripe for unabashed indulgence.

DON'T MISS

*** **Mendocino:** picturesque village set on an ocean bluff.
*** **Redwood National Park:** home of the sky-scraping redwood tree.
*** **Sonoma:** sedately paced Wine Country town with a history worth discovering.
** **Jack London State Historic Park:** former farm of the celebrated writer.
** **Fort Ross State Historic Park:** restored 19th-century Russian fur-trapping settlement.
* **Point Reyes National Seashore:** the San Andreas Fault revealed.

Opposite: *Napa Valley.*

THE COAST

The coast between San Francisco and the Oregon border holds some of California's most expressive landscapes. The narrow Highway 1 cuts a dipping and weaving – and often thrilling – course, linking tiny settlements, remote coves and inlets, and passing tiny beaches populated by barking sea lions.

Above: *The scenic coastline makes for thrilling sightseeing.*

Point Reyes National Seashore ★

The epicentre of San Francisco's 1906 earthquake was Point Reyes, 30 miles (48km) north of the city, where rolling hills give way to marshes and sand dunes in a region created by the shifts of the San Andreas Fault. **Bear Valley Visitor Center** (open Monday–Friday 09:00–17:00; weekends 08:00–17:00), signposted off Highway 1, carries the geological background. Nearby is the **Earthquake Trail**, enabling visitors to spot evidence of the 1906 earthquake – when Point Reyes moved 16ft (5m) north in an instant.

Fort Ross State Historic Park ★★

In 1812, 95 Russians arrived on a windswept headland 20 miles (32km) north of Point Reyes to hunt, trade with natives, and grow food for their fur-trapping countrymen in Alaska. The settlement lasted only 30 years but the traditional Russian buildings the settlers built from local redwood have been restored as Fort Ross State

Historic Park. The exhibits, displays, and the buildings themselves, provide an absorbing footnote in California's history (open daily 10:00–16:00). Be prepared for a loud bang at 15:00, when the Russian cannon is fired. Its blast reverberates for miles.

Mendocino ★★★

Evocatively set on a windswept bluff, the hundred-year-old clapboard cottages of Mendocino, 88 miles (142km) from Fort Ross, are maintained in the style chosen by 19th-century New England loggers who arrived to work in the local forests. An influx of writers, artists and back-to-nature types began the restoration of Mendocino through the 1960s. Efforts to preserve the past extends to not allowing fast-food outlets, petrol stations and other totems of the modern world. Tourists are welcome, though, as the many souvenir shops and bed-and-breakfast inns attest. Aimless wandering is the best way to enjoy Mendocino, but drop into the **Kelley House Museum** (open Friday, Saturday and Sundays only from September–May; daily 13:00–16:00), for its local historical collection, and the **Ford House** (open daily 11:00–16:00), the information centre for the **Mendocino Headlands State Park**, which covers the footpath-lined clifftops between the village and the raging ocean.

BUTTER PALACES

Literally as well as figuratively, the coastal town of **Eureka**, 153 miles (246km) north of Fort Bragg, was built on the 19th-century lumber trade. Unsparing use of wood created many elaborate mansions which still remain in the town. Still more artistically carpentered homes can be found in the village of **Ferndale**, just south, many of them nicknamed 'Butter Palaces' for the dairy-farm moguls who owned them.

Below: *Cattle below the snowcapped peaks in Shasta Valley.*

Above: *The Skunk train ride from Fort Bragg to Willits.*

Fort Bragg ★

Situated 2 miles (3.2km) north, Fort Bragg is Mendocino's complete opposite, a hard-working town of very ordinary appearance. The cozy lifestyle of a 19th-century lumber boss can be assessed at the **Guest House Museum**, 343 N Main Street (open Wednesday–Sunday 10:00–16:00). A better stop is the colourful array of plant life nurtured at the **Mendocino Coast Botanical Gardens**, on the town's southern approach (open daily 09:00–17:00). Fort Bragg is also one end of the **Skunk Train route** (see p. 51).

INLAND AND THE FAR NORTH COAST

Leaving San Francisco, Highway 101 navigates the lush, thickly wooded valleys that lie some 30 miles (48km) inland from the coast. As on the coastal route, settlements are few and far between but compensate for their scarcity with eccentricity: one town even has its own language. Abundant rainfall enables the region to support many redwood groves, the densest concentration being in and around Redwood National Park, north of the point where Highway 101 and Highway 1 merge.

Petaluma ★★

Petaluma, 39 miles (63km) north of San Francisco, is known in California for its dairy and poultry industry and by nostalgia movie aficionados for its well-maintained Victorian centre which featured in *Peggy Sue Got Married* and *American Graffiti*. A few hours exploration should include the **Historical Library and Museum**, 20 Fourth Street (open Sunday 13:00–16:00, Monday and Thursday–Saturday 10:00–16:00), which tackles the town's growth, and the **Petaluma Adobe State Historic Park**, beside Casa Grande Avenue on the town's outskirts (open daily 10:00–17:00). With its immense 1836 adobe building intact, the park is an evocative reminder of pre-US California and formed part of the 100 sq miles (259km²) ranch of General Mariano Vallejo, a key figure of the Mexican era though more closely linked with Sonoma (see p. 56).

(see p. 56)

BOONVILLE'S BOONTLING

Boonville is a small town between Healdsburg and Ukiah. It is home to **Boontling**, a language which evolved between the 1880s and 1920s, derived from a mixture of local anecdotes, characters and assorted words from languages spoken by immigrants. The walls of the Boonville Coffee Shop, beside Highway 101, carry a display on the strange tongue, which some of Boonville's few hundred inhabitants still speak.

Healdsburg ★

Spreading outwards from a Spanish-style plaza, Healdsburg, 38 miles (61km) from Petaluma, makes a fine picnic or lunch stop and is good news for wine fans. It boasts several wineries and the **Sonoma County Wine Library**. Inside the local library, on the corner of Center and Piper streets, this holds every volume a viticulture devotee could ever want to read. Open Monday, Wednesday 10:00–21:00; Tuesday, Thursday–Saturday 10:00–18:00.

Ukiah ★

The **Grace Hudson Museum and Sun House**, 431 Main Street, is sufficient reason to linger in Ukiah, 44 miles (70km) north of Healdsburg. Grace Hudson, who died in 1937, created many paintings of Pomo people, the native culture dominant in the region, and her husband's archaeological research contributed greatly to present-day knowledge of native Californians. A few paintings are shown here but more eye-catching are the many examples of Pomo basketry, their geometric designs replicated in the layout of the museum. Open Wednesday–Saturday 10:00–16:30, Sunday 12:00–16:30.

Willits ★

The dainty wooden railway station at Willits, 29 miles (47km) north of Ukiah, is the inland terminal of the Skunk Train, pulled by a diesel locomotive. It moves passengers along a breathtaking 40-mile (64km) route above inaccessible redwood groves between here and Fort Bragg twice daily during summer; for details, tel: (800) 866-1690.

Redwood National Park ★★★

To the north of the coastal town of Eureka, the merged highways 1 and 101 pass the southern entrance to the 110,000-acre (48,477ha) Redwood National Park. The park's main information and visitor centre is located here, providing the ecological background to the towering trees. It is also close to the easily walked **Tall Trees Trail** leading to the tallest redwood of them all: the 368ft (112m) Howard Libby Redwood.

AVENUE OF THE GIANTS

Redwood groves seldom make themselves accessible to those not prepared to leave their cars but off Highway 101 in **Humboldt Redwoods State Park**, 68 miles (109km) north of Willits, is the 33-mile (53km) route known as the Avenue of the Giants. Besides the redwood trees which rise high above it, the route brings glimpses of lush meadows and distant mountains. The park has numerous car parks from which marked foot trails lead deeper into the redwood forest.

Below: *Drive-through tree in park, Leggett – height 315ft (96m), diameter 21ft (6m) and maximum age 2400.*

MOUNT OF LEGENDS

The year-round capping of snow on its 14,162ft (4316m) summit adds to the mystique of **Mount Shasta**. The mountain is situated 8 miles (13km) east of the town of the same name on I-5 (Interstate 5). Thought by some to have been inhabited by **Lemurians**, a lost race of the Pacific, Mount Shasta has been the birthplace of countless Californian legends.

Climbing the mountain is usually possible in August but entails a strenuous full-day excursion and should only be attempted by experienced and well-equipped hikers.

Below: *The snowcapped peak of Mount Shasta.*

FAR INLAND: VOLCANO COUNTRY

Shaped by the many prehistoric (and one comparatively recent) eruptions of the volcanic **Cascade Mountains**, California's northeast corner is the least populated segment of the state. Two national parks reward the long journey needed to reach them, while the more accessible university town of Chico and the historically intriguing Weaverville stand out among the region's predominantly undistinguished communities.

Chico ★

Since its 1849 founding by the 'tall, prim and principled' John Bidwell, a settler from Missouri, Chico, 180 miles (290km) northeast of San Francisco, has been different from its neighbours. Bidwell's agricultural inventiveness brought the town highly profitable farming, while the presence of a California State University campus brings the students who help make Chico one of northern California's liveliest places for eating, drinking and making merry. Even if socializing holds little appeal, stick around long enough to visit **Bidwell Mansion State Historic Park**, 525 Esplanade Avenue. It is the site of John Bidwell's Italianate former home; the guided tours tell the absorbing tale of one of the state's most interesting and honourable pioneers. Tours daily 10:00–16:00.

Weaverville ★★

With many of its 19th-century buildings intact, Weaverville, 113 miles (182km) northwest of Chico, is a reminder of the local gold rush of the 1850s which prompted settlement in the unwelcoming hillsides of the **Browns Mountains**. Weaverville is one of the few towns of the era to last beyond the gold rush. Be sure to see the ornate **Taoist Temple**, raised by the gold-rush Chinese community, at the centre of **Joss House State Historic Park**. Open Wednesday–Sunday 10:00–17:00.

Lassen Volcanic National Park ★★★

Within a 165,000-sq-mile (427,350km²) caldera – the crater formed by the collapse of a volcano – Lassen Volcanic National Park, 80 miles (129km) north of Chico, is possessed of enough fumaroles, hot springs and pits of boiling mud to leave nobody in any doubt about the geological stresses beneath California. Many of the park's features are results of the 1915 eruption of Mount Lassen, the state's only active volcano, which sent a cloud of dust 7 miles (11km) high and smothered the surrounding land in 20ft (6m) of thick mud.

Though Lassen is unlikely to erupt again for many years, the park is proof of the ferocity of the earth's innards. The 1-mile-long (1.6km) walk to **Bumpass Hell** brings visitors as close as they dare to the park's most active hydrothermal area. It can be reached by car from the 35-mile-long (56km) road which weaves through the park's scenic highlights.

Lava Beds National Monument ★★

A thousand years ago, lava flows solidified to form the perfectly cylindrical caves which lie just beneath the ground at Lava Beds National Monument, 220 miles (354km) north of Chico. A flashlight borrowed from the visitors' centre is an essential aid in exploring the dark caves, though one, **Mushpot Cave**, is electrically lit and carries displays explaining the caves' formation.

Above: *Nature erupts in a protest of steam at Lassen Volcanic National Park.*

THE MODOC WARS

The caves of the **Lava Beds National Monument** provided the defensive positions used by 52 Modoc Indians. They fought a celebrated, but ultimately unsuccessful, action against a numerically far superior band of US troops in 1872–3.

The Modoc Wars lasted five months, as the natives resisted forced resettlement.

Evidence of the area's importance in prehistoric civilization is illustrated by its many petroglyphs and rock paintings, the most impressive of which can be seen inside **Big Painted Cave**.

Right: *Napa Valley wineries: Beringer and Sterling Vineyards.*

THE WINE COUNTRY

Wineries are found all over California but it is the 300 secreted throughout the **Napa** and **Sonoma** valleys – the so-called Wine Country, an hour's drive from San Francisco – that gain most respect. The wineries attract several million visitors annually to their tours and tastings. Napa is by far the most visited of the two valleys; Sonoma makes a very relaxing alternative, its wineries fewer but no less satisfying.

Touring the Napa Valley

Despite giving its name to California's most commercially important wine producing valley, the town of Napa grew rapidly as a transportation hub – moving wine along the **Napa River** to San Francisco – rather than as a wine-making centre. While 60,000 inhabitants make it easily the largest valley community, Napa holds little of consequence beyond a plethora of lovingly restored Victorian homes and pleasant river-side pathways.

Of greater note is **Domaine Chandon**, 5 miles (8km) north of Napa in Yountville, opened by the renowned French company Möet et Chandon in 1986 and now producing 500,000 cases of sparkling wine each year. Guided tours divulge the secrets of *méthode champenoise* (the tra-

---

R.L. STEVENSON'S NAPA VALLEY

In 1880, Scottish writer Robert Louis Stevenson and his Oakland-born bride enjoyed a low-budget honeymoon in an abandoned silver miners' hut in what is now **Robert Louis Stevenson State Park**, just north of Calistoga off Highway 29. The visit there gave rise to Stevenson's story, *The Silverado Squatters*. The view of **Mount St Helena**, on whose slopes the park sits, are said to have inspired the landscapes of the writer's subsequent *Treasure Island*.

ditional way of making sparkling wine) and the heady elixir can be sampled from the champagne bar and café.

Most Napa wineries are clustered around Oakville, Rutherford and St Helena in the heart of the valley. At the smaller operations, such as **Silver Oak Cellars**, 915 Oakville Cross Road, and **Grgich Hills**, 1829 St Helena Highway, specializing in Cabernet Sauvignon and Chardonnay respectively, visitors may find the owner on hand for an informal chat. If wine appreciation is a total mystery, however, aim for **Robert Mondavi Winery**, 7801 St Helena Highway, where 75-minute tours lift the lid on Californian viticulture and the fine points of wine tasting.

Some of the best views of the vine-cloaked valley are from the aerial cable car which provides access to **Sterling Vineyards**, sited on a knoll 300ft (91m) above Dunawell Lane, just south of Calistoga. After the ascent, there is ample opportunity to sample the winery's products and further relish the outlook.

Below: *Youngsters picking grapes in the Napa Valley.*

Calistoga effectively marks the end of the valley and of the wineries. Founded by the colourful Sam Brannan (*see* p. 16) in 1859 as a spa resort, Calistoga has been exploiting the mineral-rich volcanic mud of nearby Mount St Helena ever since. Countless resort hotels offer mud-bath and massage packages to ease the aches of stress-afflicted Californians.

Geothermal phenomena litter Calistoga's surrounds. The **Old Faithful Geyser**, 1 mile (1.6km) north, sends a jet of scalding water skywards one to three times an hour. Less dramatic but much more curious is the **Petrified Forest**, 5 miles (8km) west on Petrified Forest Road, where chemicals in volcanic ash turned a prehistoric grove of redwoods to stone.

Mr Greenfingers

Amid the housing estates and shopping malls of **Santa Rosa**, at the northern end of the Sonoma Valley, the **Luther Burbank Memorial Gardens**, 204 Santa Rosa Avenue, celebrate the man whose horticultural skills created 800 new varieties of flower, fruit and vegetables. Burbank arrived in California in 1875 with just 10 potatoes to his name. His remarkable tale is outlined in the guided tours and in a small museum.

Below: *The unusual Ravenswood wine label.*

Touring the Sonoma Valley

Relaxed Sonoma could hardly provide a better introduction to the valley which bears its name or set a mood so well-suited to exploring the valley, its wines, and Sonoma's own place in Californian history. The site of the state's northernmost mission – uncompleted as control of California switched from Spain to Mexico – Sonoma became the base of one of California's major Mexican-era landowners, General Mariano Vallejo. It was Vallejo who gave Sonoma its 8-acre (3ha) plaza, on the north side of which stands the unprepossessing **Mission San Francisco Solano** and the **Sonoma Barracks**, a garrison for Vallejo's troops now stuffed with memorabilia of the short-lived Bear Flag Republic (*see p. 15*). Their restoration continuing, both buildings form part of the **Sonoma State Historic Park** (open daily 10:00–17:00), as does Mariano Vallejo's house, **Lachryma Montis**, holding the general's furnishings and belongings and which gives a pithy account of the ups and downs of life in 19th-century California.

Sonoma saw the state's first commercial winery, the **Buena Vista Winery**, founded in 1857 by Agoston Haraszthy and now occupying an immensely picnic-worthy setting 2 miles (3.2km) from the town centre on Old Winery Road.

In Sonoma itself, **Sebastiani Vineyards**, 398 Fourth Street East, has excellent wines and tours. Anyone who believes the typical wine snob's comment that Zinfandel, a grape that originated in the USA, cannot make a good wine, will be pleasantly surprised by the quality Zinfandels created at **Ravenswood**, 18701 Gehricke Road.

Little more than a group of houses and shops around a bend in Arnold Drive (running parallel to Highway 12 from Sonoma), **Glen Ellen** marks the junction off which Jack London Ranch Road rises steeply to the former home of Jack London, the successful Oakland-born writer (author of *Call of the Wild* and *The Sea Wolf* among others) who moved here in 1913.

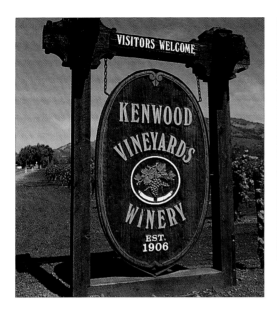

Left: *Visitors are invited to sample the wines.*

The 800-acre (324ha) **Jack London State Historic Park** preserves the site of London's ranch and the remains of the 26-room **Wolf House**, destroyed by fire shortly before its completion as a home for the author and his wife. The **House of Happy Walls** holds items from London's life and work and provides incentive to follow the short trails leading to the Wolf House's ruins and London's grave site. The writer died here in 1916. Park open daily 08:00–17:00 or 19:00; buildings daily 10:00–17:00.

At **Kenwood**, 10 miles (16km) from Sonoma on Highway 12 or reachable on the meandering Warms Spring Road from Glen Ellen, **Chateau St Jean**, 8555 Sonoma Highway, occupies a would-be French château and deserves its reputation for top-notch Chardonnay.

The valley's verdant countryside may well exert as strong an influence as the local wines. Set across facing hillsides, **Annadel** and **Sugarloaf Ridge state parks** rise from woodlands into rugged scrub-covered ridges. They are criss-crossed by walking, hiking and horse-riding trails and populated by deer, bobcats and squirrels.

Northern California and the Wine Country at a Glance

Northern California endures some of the heaviest **rainfall** in the USA, dense coastal fog, and winter temperatures which can drop well below freezing point. Although the coastal fog may persist, **May** to **September** brings the sunniest and driest conditions, though evenings are often cool. Wine Country conditions are much less severe year-round, though the popularity of the region, particularly the Napa Valley in summer, causes **October** to **May** to be the least congested and most pleasurable time for touring.

The coast and inland are both easily reached with Highway 101 from San Francisco, off which branches Highway 1. Chico, in the far north, is a three- to four-hour **drive** from San Francisco via I-80 and I-5 (Interstate highways). The Wine Country valleys are adjacent to one another, an hour's drive from San Francisco via Highway 101 or I-80. Public transport is very sketchy although **buses** do have a limited service to Napa and Sonoma from Sacramento.

A region of long distances and wide open spaces with few non-local public transport connections, Northern California is virtually impossible to see without a **car**.

The Coast
LUXURY
Stanford Inn by the Sea, Mendocino, tel: (707) 937-5615, fax: (707) 937-0305. Fully equipped rooms.

MID-RANGE
Grey Whale Inn, 615 N Main Street, Fort Bragg, tel: (707) 964-0640, fax: (707) 964-4408. A bed-and-breakfast inn.

BUDGET
Surf Motel, 1220 S Main Street, Fort Bragg, tel: (707) 964-5361, fax: (707) 964-3187. Pick of the town's motels.

Inland
LUXURY
Madrona Manor, 1001 Westside Road, Healdsburg, tel: (707) 433-4231, fax: (707) 433-0703. Bed-and-breakfast inn.

MID-RANGE
Best Western Petaluma Inn, 200 S McDowell Boulevard, Petaluma, tel: (707) 763-0994, fax: (707) 778-3111. Reliable.

BUDGET
Rodeway Inn, 1050 S State Street, Ukiah, tel: (707) 462-2906, fax: (707) 462-3040. Clean, simple and central.

Far Inland: Volcano Country
MID-RANGE
Grateful Bed, 1462 Arcadian Avenue, Chico, tel: (530) 342-2464. Bed and breakfast in a 1905 home.

L'abri Bed and Breakfast, 14350 Highway 99, Chico, tel: (530) 489-3319, fax: (530) 895-0735. Pleasant rustic retreat on the outskirts of town.

BUDGET
Safari Inn, 2352 Esplanade, Chico, tel: (530) 343-3201. Plain and simple motel.

Wine Country
LUXURY
Sonoma Mission Inn & Spa, 18140 Sonoma Highway, Sonoma, tel: (707) 938-9000, fax: (707) 938-4250. Perfect place to be wrapped in seaweed, just one of the many spa treatments available.
Auberge du Soleil, 180 Rutherford Hill Road, Rutherford, tel: (707) 963-1211, fax: (707) 963-8764. Decadent French-style villas.

MID-RANGE
El Dorado Inn, 405 First Street West, Sonoma, tel: (707) 996-3220, fax: (707) 996-3148. In town, overlooking the plaza.
Rancho Caymus Inn, 1140 Rutherford Road, Rutherford, tel: (707) 963-1777, fax: (707) 963-5387. Beautifully designed property.

The Coast
LUXURY
Café Beaujolais, 961 Ukiah Street, Mendocino, tel: (707) 937-5614. Brick-oven-baked pizzas served for lunch and special creations for dinner.

MID-RANGE

Mendo Bistro, 300 N Main Street, Fort Bragg, tel: (707) 964-4974. Excellent seafood and pasta dishes.

Mendocino Café, 10451 Lansing Street, Mendocino, tel: (707) 937-6141. Inventive mix of Asian and American dishes.

North Coast Brewing Company, 4455 N Main Street, Fort Bragg, tel: (707) 964-BREW. Pasta and seafood dinners and own-brew beers.

BUDGET

Egghead's Restaurant, 326 N Main Street, Fort Bragg, tel: (707) 964-5005. Offers 40 varieties of omelettes and more.

Inland

LUXURY

Madrona Manor Restaurant, Healdsburg (*see* p. 58). Known for the flair and inventiveness of the chef and elegance of the setting.

MID-RANGE

Graziano's, 170 Petaluma Boulevard, Petaluma, tel: (707) 762-5997. Reliable Italian fare, served for dinner only.

Bella Luma, 125 Petaluma Boulevard N, Petaluma, tel: (707) 762-2004. Cosy spot for Italian fare.

BUDGET

Dempsey's Alehouse, 50 E Washington Street, Petaluma, tel: (707) 765-9694. Beers brewed on premises. Serves burgers and chicken wings.

Far Inland: Volcano Country

MID-RANGE

Spice Creek Café, 230 W Third Street, Chico, tel: (530) 891-9951. Creative and eclectic menu.

BUDGET

The Brewery Restaurant, 401 S Main Street, Weaverville, tel: (530) 623-3000. Delicious breakfasts and lunches.

Moxie's Café, 128 Broadway, Chico, tel: (530) 345-0601. Gourmet coffee and teas and tasty soups and sandwiches. Live jazz on weekend nights.

Sierra Nevada Brewing Company, 1075 E 20th Street, Chico, tel: (530) 345-2739. Fine selection of microbrewed ales.

Franky's, 506 Ivy Street, Chico, tel: (530) 898-9947. Tasty pizza and pasta dishes.

Wine Country

LUXURY

Tra Vigne, 1050 Charter Oak Avenue, St Helena, tel: (707) 963-4444. Exquisite California variations on Tuscany-influenced food.

Mustard's Grill, 7399 St Helena Highway, Yountville, tel: (707) 944 2424. A pace setter for gourmet eating.

MID-RANGE

Della Santina's, 101 E Napa Street, Sonoma, tel: (707) 935-0576. Northern Italian cuisine served inside or out.

The Red Grape, 529 First Street W, Sonoma, tel: (707)

996-4103. Pizza and pasta, served inside or out.

Tours and Excursions

Hot-air balloons are only a slightly less common sight than wineries in the Napa Valley. Balloon rides are offered by several companies, among them the **Bonaventure Balloon Company**, tel: (1-800) FLY-NAPA, and **Napa Valley Balloons**, tel: (1-800) 253-2224 or (707) 944-0228.

Useful Contacts

Bear Valley Visitor Center, tel: (415) 464-5100, www.nps.gov/pore/index.htm

Fort Ross State Historic Park, tel: (707) 847-3286, www.parks.ca.gov

Petaluma Visitor Center, 210 Lakeview Street, tel: (1-877) 273-8258, fax: (707) 769-0429, www.visitpetaluma.com

Redwood National Park, tel: (707) 464-6101, www.nps.gov/redw

Lava Beds National Monument, tel: (916) 667-1800, www.nps.gov/labe

Lassen Volcanic National Park, tel: (916) 595-4444, www.nps.gov/lavo

Napa Valley Convention and Visitors Bureau, 1310 Napa Town Centre, Napa, tel: (707) 226-7459, www.napavalley.org

Sonoma County Tourism Bureau, 420 Aviation Boulevard, Santa Rosa, tel: toll free 1-800 576-6662, fax: (707) 539-7252.

4
Gold Country and the Sierra Nevada

Gold made California a rich and powerful state and it is no accident that its capital, **Sacramento**, 87 miles (140km) east of San Francisco, stands at the gateway to the Gold Country, site of the major finds. Sacramento is an ideal taster for a region where the gold rush still seems a recent memory. Scores of towns raised in the boom years survive along Highway 49, some 35 miles (56km) east of Sacramento. Their false-fronted buildings and raised sidewalks are zealously maintained by residents, many of whom moved to these once raucous but now peaceful environs to escape the hurly-burly of the coastal cities.

All roads east of Sacramento climb steadily into the **Sierra Nevada**, the mountains forming California's spine which provided the final obstacle to 19th-century travellers from the Eastern USA. The mountains' western slopes rise gently and are covered by groves of cedar and oak that ascend into thick belts of pine and fir. In this verdant landscape sits **Lake Tahoe**, a vast expanse of cobaltblue water. Further south, **Yosemite National Park** spreads across a sizeable chunk of the Sierra Nevada but is best known for **Yosemite Valley**, a meadow lubricated by waterfalls tumbling down immense walls of granite.

Crossing to the eastern side of the mountains brings complete change. Highway 395 cuts through an area possessed of extraordinary phenomena: **Mono Lake** and its tufa formations, the geometrically precise lava cylinders of the **Devil's Postpile Monument**, and the 4000-year-old trees of the **Ancient Bristlecone Pine Forest**.

DON'T MISS

*** **Lake Tahoe:** the USA's largest alpine lake.
*** **California State Railroad Museum:** wonderful stash of locos and insights into California's past.
*** **Yosemite National Park:** natural California at its best.
*** **Mono Lake:** placid body of water fringed with otherwordly tufa formations.
** **Donner Memorial State Park:** site of pioneer-era tragedy and Donner Lake.
* **Columbia:** preserved and restored gold-rush town.

Opposite: *Merced River in Yosemite National Park.*

Above: *The State Capitol, seen from its gardens.*

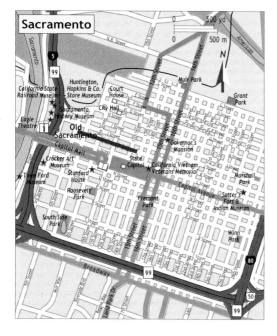

SACRAMENTO AND VICINITY

There are few better places to get a grip on California's past than Sacramento, state capital and gateway to the **Gold Country**, and a city that blossomed as the state soared from backwater to economic powerhouse. Nearby, **Folsom** provides a further appetizer for the Gold Country while the **Sacramento Delta** is a backwoods area of meandering waterways and minuscule communities.

Sacramento ★★★

California's capital since 1854, Sacramento is a small and easily explored city despite being the centre of decision-making in one of the country's most powerful states. The political battles are fought within the majestic neoclassical **State Capitol** building, topped by a 210ft-high (64m) rotunda completed in 1872. Free guided tours of the State Capitol begin on the hour (details from the basement information office) and are necessary if the building is to reveal its secrets; otherwise the re-created offices from the early 1900s and the portraits of former governors lining the walls seem very pedestrian.

A 15-minute walk east, **Old Town Sacramento** holds 100 restored buildings from the 1850s, when the Sacramento River made the city a supply centre for the gold mines. Several fine museums vie for attention amid restaurants and souvenir shops, and include the **California State Railroad Museum**, 111 I Street (open daily 10:00–17:00), a lively collection of ageing locos and carriages confirming the importance of railways to California's growth and the rise of the Big Four (see p. 17). A broader sweep of Sacramento's back pages is provided next door by the engrossing **Sacramento Discovery Museum**, 101 I Street (open Tuesday–Sunday 10:00–16:30) which includes re-created gold rush-era storefronts and much on the contribution of the Chinese to California's economic rise.

Folsom ★

More than a tenth of Folsom's 65,000 population live within the stern granite

Above: *Getting around in Old Town Sacramento.*

walls of the town's prison, immortalized in song by Johnny Cash in the 1950s and still the community's best-known feature. Chronicling all manner of wrongdoing and brutality, the prison museum wields a macabre appeal. Folsom itself, 22 miles (35km) east of Sacramento on Highway 50, is a far more wholesome place. The town is a gold-rush survivor with a fine stash of ageing knickknacks filling its **History Museum**, 823 Sutter Street, inside the 1860 Wells Fargo building (open Tuesday–Sunday 11:00–16:00).

The Sacramento Delta ★

One of California's best-kept secrets is the Sacramento Delta, into which Northern California's three major rivers flow and mingle around 70 small islands. The delta is explored at somnambulant pace by in-the-know tourists in houseboats and by drivers on Highway 160, also known as the Delta Highway. It has few specific sights save for the near-abandoned communities of Chinese labourers who built the delta's canals and levees in the early 1900s. The place to head for is **Locke**, where the **Dai Loy Museum** recalls the days of opium dens, brothels and illicit gambling (open weekends 12:00–15:00).

LAKE TAHOE AND VICINITY

The cool blue waters of Lake Tahoe sit 6223ft (1897m) above sea level, fringed by forests of fir and pine and over-looked by bold granite peaks rising above 9000ft (2743m).

SUTTER'S FORT

Sacramento sits on the former land of **John Sutter**, a German-born immigrant who wheedled a 48,000-acre (19,425ha) land grant out of California's then Mexican rulers in 1839. His base, Sutter's Fort, became a major supply centre as the initial gold discovery was made on his land. But the gold rush proved to be his downfall as his workers abandoned their jobs to seek their fortunes while new arrivals squatted on his land. At the junction of 27th and L streets, Sutter's Fort's adobe buildings have been restored and period-attired guides provide visitors with a historical commentary.

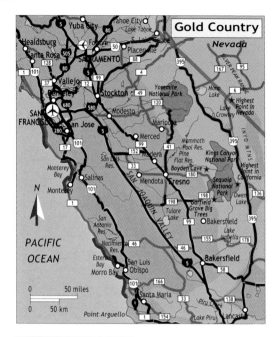

Gold Country

Around the 72 miles (116km) of shoreline, a third of which lies within Nevada, are state parks, small towns and every opportunity to savour the largest alpine lake in the USA.

Donner Memorial State Park ★★

Beside I-80, 110 miles (177km) east of Sacramento, Donner Memorial State Park might look like a beautiful place for a picnic, framed by pine trees and holding the blue expanse of **Lake Donner**, but it actually marks one of early California's greatest tragedies. In 1846, the Donner Party – a wagon train of 89 men, women and children from the American East – became stranded by early snowfalls as they tried to cross what is now Donner Pass. Without food, 40 of the party perished during the winter, some of the survivors resorting to cannibalism to stay alive. The park's **Emigrant Trail Museum** records the grim event and outlines the many perils faced by California-bound travellers of the mid-1800s (open daily 09:00–16:00).

Tahoe City ★

Approaching from the west, diminutive Tahoe City, straddling the junction of highways 89 and 28, brings the first close-up sight of Lake Tahoe. In the 1910s, efforts to dam the lake's only river, the **Truckee**, failed but one of the abandoned dam buildings became the **Gatekeeper's Museum** and **Marion Steinbach Indian Basket Museum**. It is packed with displays and information on local native cultures and wildlife. Open daily 11:00–17:00.

Sugar Pine Point State Park ★★

Beside Highway 89,8 miles (13km) south of Tahoe City, Sugar Pine Point State Park is a mix of slender beaches and woodlands. Its visitors' centre is inside the 1903 **Erhmann Mansion**, a reminder of the days when Lake Tahoe was considered the private domain of California's great and good.

South Lake Tahoe ★★

With motels, restaurants, and car and boat rental outlets by the score along Highway 50 (known locally as South Lake Tahoe Boulevard), South Lake Tahoe is by far the most commercially developed lakeside community. The lake is seldom more than a few minutes stroll away and a westward amble along its banks finds the **Tallac Historic Site**. The site is a series of opulent summer homes built for wealthy Californians in the 1920s (open daily mid-June–mid-September 10:00–16:00). Above South Lake Tahoe, the slopes of **Heavenly Valley** test the skills of advanced skiers in winter. During summer the resort's aerial tram hoists visitors to the hillside restaurant and to the foot trails which bring astounding panoramas of Lake Tahoe and its surrounds from over 8000ft (2438m) up. For many, however, the natural setting is less appealing than the proximity of the state of Nevada where gambling is legal. In South Lake Tahoe's twin city of **Stateline**, anyone who fancies their chances can take their pick of several sparkling casinos.

Touring Highway 49: Placerville to Mariposa

Highway 49 links many of the Gold Country communities which had their start in 1849, the peak year of the gold rush. Some became ruins but others survived and now their false-fronted buildings, raised sidewalks, and countryside setting make them extremely attractive. The section detailed here makes a simple link between Placerville, 37 miles (60km) east of Sacramento, and Yosemite National Park, 45 miles (72km) east of Mariposa.

Placerville was known in its early days as 'Hangtown', allegedly for the townsfolks' propensity to administer summary justice. The **El Dorado County Historical Museum** displays mining machinery by the tonne (open Wednesday–

Lake Tahoe Cruises

Two Mississippi paddle-wheel steamboats make regular trips of a few hours duration across Lake Tahoe to Emerald Bay and back.
The Tahoe Queen departs from South Lake Tahoe, and the **MS Dixie** from Zephyr Cove, 3 miles (5km) north of Stateline. For information and reservations tel: (888) 896-3830.

Below: *Lake Tahoe, seen from its encircling mountains and at Emerald Bay.*

Above: *The arid beauty of Big Pine Creek in the Sierra Nevada mountains.*

Saturday 10:00–16:00; Sunday 12:00–16:00). For eating, daring diners might sample 'hangtown fry', a local speciality of scrambled eggs, bacon and fried oysters apparently resulting from a condemned man's last request.

Legend has it that at **Angels Camp**, 62 miles (100km) further south, an overheard conversation inspired writer Mark Twain to write his short story, *The Celebrated Jumping Frog of Caleveras County*, also the title of his first published collection. With Twain having become an established part of US literary history, Angels Camp decided to celebrate the connection, in 1928, by holding the first of its now-annual **Jumping Frog Festivals**. Visit during May and you will see the town bedecked with frog-related paraphernalia.

The most complete gold rush town is **Columbia**, 17 miles (27km) from Angels Camp. It is actually a state historic park preserving and restoring many of the town's original buildings to working order: the restaurant serves food, the hotel offers accommodation, and period-attired individuals wax lyrical on the pleasures and pains of gold-rush life.

To show that local justice was no longer the preserve of the lynch mob, Gold Country communities often gave themselves grandiose courthouses, one of the better examples being the white pine affair at **Mariposa**, 63 miles (101km) further on. Mariposa's greatest asset, however, is the **Mariposa Museum and History Center**, which provides an engrossing and detailed documentation of the gold-rush era (open daily in summer 10:00–16:00; weekends only rest of year).

THE NATIONAL PARKS AND THE EASTERN SIERRA

The **Sierra Nevada** mountains dominate the view throughout the **Gold Country**. Secreted within their forested foothills are three national parks, including Yosemite which should be on every California visitor's itinerary. Across the mountains lie the very different landscapes of the Eastern Sierra. Much of the rest of the 1200-sq-mile (3109km²) park can be explored only on demanding hiking trails.

Yosemite National Park ★★★

The destination for 80% of Yosemite National Park's 3.9 million annual visitors is the 7-mile-long (11km), 1-mile-wide (1.6km) **Yosemite Valley**, where natural California makes its most eloquent statement. Meandering streams, lush meadows and woodlands comprise the valley floor while sheer granite walls, rising 3000ft (914m) above and rippled by waterfalls, form its sides. The gorgeous valley holds the park's main visitor services and is the starting-point of a number of trails: easy ones to the glass-like **Mirror Lake** and to **Lower Yosemite Falls**, and steeper treks of several hours duration to **Upper Yosemite Falls** and to **Vernal** and **Nevada falls**. More strenuous still is the 4-mile (6km) uphill hike to **Glacier Point** and a view of the valley from 3200ft (975m) above.

A STUNNING PASS

Yosemite National Park's summer-only **Tioga Pass Road**, a continuation of Highway 120, penetrates the High Sierra wilderness to reach alpine Tuolumune Meadows, 8575ft (2614m) above sea level, before descending towards Highway 395 and the Eastern Sierra.

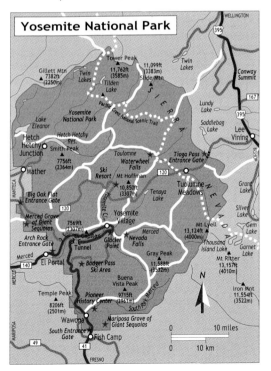

Yosemite National Park

THE MARIPOSA GROVE

If you are not heading for Kings Canyon and Sequoia National Parks (see p. 68) do not pass up the chance to visit Yosemite's Mariposa Grove. It is situated 2 miles (3km) from the park's south entrance on Highway 41 and 36 miles (58km) from the valley. The grove holds the biggest and best of Yosemite's 3000-year-old **giant sequoia trees**.

DEVIL'S POSTPILE NATIONAL MONUMENT

Between Mono Lake and Bishop, turning east off Highway 395 on to Highway 203, leads into the ski-resort town of **Mammoth Lakes**. From the town, Minaret Road continues into the mountains and connects with a simple foot trail leading to the **Devil's Postpile National Monument**. It's a spectacular stack of hexagonal-shaped basalt created as molten lava from **Mammoth Mountain** cooled and fractured and was smoothed by glacial action.

Kings Canyon and Sequoia National Parks ★★

Scenic drives, caves and meadows all feature in the combined Kings Canyon and Sequoia National Parks but the focus of attention are the latter's giant sequoia groves. Related to the coastal redwoods, growing less tall but much stouter, the giant sequoias are the world's largest living things. With a base circumference of 102ft (31m), the biggest of them all is the **General Sherman Tree**, signposted just north of the visitors' centre at Giant Forest.

The Eastern Sierra ★★

With arid, treeless valleys at the foot of 10,000ft-high (3048m) peaks and a smattering of small towns, the Eastern Sierra provides great contrasts to the mountains' western side. Highway 395 is the only road through the area and it meets Tioga Pass Road close to **Lee Vining**.

A remnant of a prehistoric sea with no natural drainage, **Mono Lake**, immediately north of **Lee Vining**, has become heavily saline. Its falling water level – due to the damming of its feeder streams to provide water for Los Angeles – has exposed strangely shaped tufa formations on its southeastern edge. The tufa, and the lake's complex ecology, is explained in depth at the **Mono Basin Scenic Area Visitors' Center** beside Highway 395 (open daily 09:00–16:30; reduced opening in winter).

Below: Tufa formations exposed by Mono Lake's falling water level.

Highway 168, off Highway 395, 80 miles (129km) south of **Lee Vining**, leads into the **Ancient Bristlecone Pine Forest**, where 4000-year-old bristlecone pines (*see* p. 10) live out their unhurried existence.

Independence, 43 miles (69km) south on Highway 395, holds the highly commendable **Eastern Sierra Museum**, 155 Grant Street (open Wednesday–Monday 10:00 –16:00) exploring the ethnic and cultural life of the region and carrying an extensive account of the Manzanar relocation camp, where 10,000 Japanese-Americans were interned during World War II. The Manzanar National Historic site lies just south of the town.

Gold Country and The Sierra Nevada at a Glance

Best Times to Visit

Sacramento endures hot and humid summers and usually mild winters. Closer to the mountains one can experience freezing winters.

Getting There

Sacramento has strong **air**, **bus** and **rail** links across the state. There are bus links from Reno airport (in Nevada) to Stateline (for South Lake Tahoe). A single daily Greyhound service travels the Eastern Sierra's Highway 395 between Reno and Los Angeles. Highway 395 can be reached on minor roads from South Lake Tahoe, or (in summer) with Highway 120 through Yosemite National Park.

Getting Around

Local buses serve Sacramento and parts of Lake Tahoe in summer. Comprehensive touring can only be done by **car**.

Where to Stay

Sacramento and Vicinity
MID-RANGE
Delta King, 1000 Front Street, Sacramento, tel: (916) 444-5464, fax: (916) 444-5314. Converted paddle-steamer.

Lake Tahoe and Vicinity
LUXURY
Harrah's Lake Tahoe, Highway 50, Stateline, tel: (702) 588-6611, fax: 588-6607. One of the best casino-hotels.

MID-RANGE
Inn by the Lake, 3300 Lake Tahoe Boulevard, South Lake Tahoe, tel: (530) 542-0330, fax: 541-6596. Comfortable rooms opposite the lake.

National Parks
LUXURY
Ahwanee, Yosemite Valley, Yosemite National Park, tel: (559) 253-5636, fax: (559) 456-0542. Lavish and lovely.
MID-RANGE
Yosemite Lodge, Yosemite Valley, Yosemite National Park, tel: (559) 253-5636, fax: (559) 456-0542. Comfortable, in the heart of the valley.

Where to Eat

Sacramento and Vicinity
LUXURY
Waterboy, 2000 Capitol Avenue, Sacramento, tel: (916) 498-9891. California-style lunch and dinner.
MID-RANGE
California Fat's, 1015 Front Street, Sacramento, tel: (916) 441-7966. An eclectic West Coast menu.
BUDGET
Rubicon Brewing Company, 2004 Capitol Avenue, Sacramento, tel: (916) 448-7032. Home-brewed beers and an array of filling meals.

Lake Tahoe and Vicinity
MID-RANGE
The Fresh Ketch, 2433 Venice Drive E, South Lake Tahoe, tel: (530) 541-5683. Seafood in generous portions.

BUDGET
Sprouts, 3125 Harrison Avenue, tel: (530) 541-6969. Healthy and predominantly vegetarian.

National Parks
LUXURY
Ahwanee Dining Room, as hotel left, reservation essential, tel: (209) 372-1489. Excellent food, views to match.
MID-RANGE
Mountain Room, Yosemite Lodge, Yosemite National Park, tel: (559) 253-5635. Hearty lunches and dinners.
BUDGET
Degnan's Café, Yosemite Lodge, Yosemite National Park, tel: (559) 253-5635. Buffet-style soup & salad.

Useful Contacts

Sacramento Convention and Visitors Bureau, 1608 I Street, tel: (916) 808-7777.
South Lake Tahoe Chamber of Commerce, 3066 Highway 50, tel: (530) 541-5255.
Yosemite National Park, tel: (559) 372-0200 and **hotel reservations**, tel: (559) 253-5635. Camping reservations, tel: toll free 1-800 436-7275.
Yosemite road and weather, tel: (559) 372-0200.
Yosemite sightseeing tours, tel: (559) 658-TOUR.
Sequoia and Kings Canyon National Parks, tel: (559) 565-3341.
Mono Basin Scenic Area Visitors Center, Lee Vining, tel: (760) 646-3044.

5
The Central Coast

California's Central Coast is an obvious route between San Francisco and Los Angeles but could hardly be a greater contrast to the state's two major cities. For some 300 miles (483km) the outlook is predominantly one of nature: **Pacific** waves crash against rocky headlands which jut from the scrub-covered slopes of coastal mountains and sea lions are a more common sight than sunbathers on many of the beaches scattered infrequently through the region.

Several hours of driving separate the Central Coast's major centres of population and everywhere the pace is unhurried and the mood relaxed. With many villages dependent on fishing, seafood is regarded with an almost religious fervour and is served in portions which are rarely other than large and fresh. Wine also has a high profile, with several noted **vineyards** secreted in the sunny valleys of the Central Coast's more southerly reaches.

Despite its abiding sense of emptiness, the Central Coast has a colourful past. It was here that the colonizing **Spanish** of the 18th century had their Californian headquarters and it was from the region's sheltered harbours that they explored and named much of the Californian coast. Some 150 years after the first Spaniards arrived, the immeasurably rich William Randolph Hearst chose an isolated Central Coast site to erect **Hearst Castle**: one of the most extravagant homes California has ever seen and which now draws more visitors than other any tourist attraction in the state except Disneyland®.

DON'T MISS

*** Big Sur: the Californian coast at its most stunning.
*** Hearst Castle: former home of multi-millionaire William Randolph Hearst.
*** Santa Barbara: the epitome of a Southern Californian town.
** Carmel Mission: the prettiest mission of all.
* La Purisima Mission State Historic Park: comprehensively restored mission complex.

Opposite: *Isolated sands seen on the route between Carmel and Gorda.*

Central Coast

Monterey Bay
Watsonville
Castroville
Pacific Grove
Asiloma
Carmel
Monterey
Point Lobos
State Reserve
Salinas
Point Sur
101
SIERRA DE SALINAS
Big Sur
Soledad

0   20 miles
0   20 km

King City

Jolon
San
Antonio
Res.
Hearst
Castle
101
San Simeon
Cambria
Nacimiento
Res.
Paso Robles
Point Estero
46   46
Cayucos
Atascadero
41   Atascadero
Morro Bay
Morro Bay
State Park
Pt Buchon
58
Pt San Luis
San Luis
Obispo
227
Pismo
Beach
Arroyo
Grande
Guadalupe   101
Point Sal   Twitchell
La Res.
Oak Knolls   Santa   166
Maria
Los
Alamos
La Purisima
Mission State
Historic Park
154
Solvang
Gaviota   Santa Ynez
Gaviota   Lake
Cachuma
Refugio   1
Isla Vista
Santa
Barbara

SANTA CRUZ, THE MONTEREY PENINSULA AND BIG SUR

Approaching from San Francisco, the first settlement of notable size on the Central Coast is the relaxed and enjoyable Santa Cruz, which sits on the northern edge of the gently curving Monterey Bay. Often visible from **Santa Cruz**, the Monterey Peninsula marks the southern end of the bay and holds the three distinct communities of **Monterey**, **Pacific Grove** and **Carmel**. The mixture of coastal views and Californian history – Monterey was the region's earliest capital while Carmel holds one of the state's prettiest Spanish missions – makes the peninsula a likely base for a one- or two-day stay. Some of the smaller but easily reached inland towns also merit a look before continuing along the coast to the wild vistas of **Big Sur**.

Santa Cruz ★

Anyone lured to California by its associations with surfing should pay respects to Santa Cruz's clifftop **Surfing Museum** (open Wednesday–Monday 12:00–16:00; closed Wednesday in winter), a one-room collection devoted to the sport. Santa Cruz is one of the few northern Californian coastal towns where conditions are often ideal for surfing. Novices and experts alike can regularly be seen cresting the local waves; the footpath winding along the clifftops makes an excellent vantage point.

Santa Cruz's appealingly hedonistic mood is aided by the roller-coaster, rifle ranges and other fairground attrac-

Right: *Santa Cruz, a beach town, is popular with sunbathers and water-sports enthusiasts.*

tions of the beachside **Boardwalk**, and the many students of the local branch of the University of California, its campus set with the redwood forests which flank the town. The presence of the students is partly responsible for the town's impressive endowment of informal and inexpensive places to eat, drink and socialize.

Since the 1791 **Santa Cruz Mission** (open Tuesday–Saturday 10:00–16:00; Sunday 10:00–14:00) is remembered only by a disappointing replica (the original having been destroyed by an earthquake in the mid-19th century), spare time is better spent enjoying the undemanding **Mystery Spot** (open daily 09:00–17:00), a series of optical illusions in a redwood grove. You can also visit the **Roaring Camp and Big Trees Railroad**, whose steam locomotive drags open carriages giddily into the hills, providing passengers with breathtaking views of the town and the coast.

Monterey ★★

Monterey is a potent reminder of the California of the Spanish, Mexican and early USA eras. The commendable **Path of History** (in **Monterey State Historic Park**) traces a route through the settlement that was chosen in 1770 as the major Spanish base in California, on account of its harbour and strategic location. The path passes numerous early adobe buildings and other historic structures, including 530 Houston Street, where Scottish writer Robert Louis Stevenson stayed for a few weeks in 1879. It is alleged to be the most haunted building in the state.

More evidence of the past is displayed at the **Maritime Museum of Monterey** (open Thursday–Tuesday 10:00–17:00), and the adjacent **Custom Hall (House)** (hours as museum), stacked floor to ceiling with ship's cargo typical of that which would have been unloaded here in the early 19th century.

From the early 1900s, Monterey led the world in **sardine canning**, tinning 250,000 tonnes of the fish

Below: *A quiet neighbourhood in Monterey.*

annually in the waterfront factories of **Cannery Row**. In its original form, Cannery Row inspired John Steinbeck's downbeat novel of the same name but with sardine stocks exhausted by the mid-forties, the industry faded and the shacks of **Cannery Row** now hold mostly busy but lacklustre souvenir shops, snack bars and cafés.

At the western end of Cannery Row, however, the state-of-the-art **Monterey Bay Aquarium** provides an outstanding introduction to the mysteries of life beneath the ocean waves, holding over 6000 of the creatures found amid the deep reefs, rocky shores and tidepools of the Californian coastline. Open daily 09:30–18:00.

Pacific Grove ★

Aside from the attractive wood-framed Victorian buildings along Lighthouse Avenue and the small but informative **Museum of Natural History** (open Tuesday–Saturday 10:00–17:00), much of Pacific Grove is unrewarding residential territory. But walking, cycling or driving along the aptly named Ocean View Boulevard, which curves around the western edge of the peninsula close to the dainty **Point Piños Lighthouse** (open Thursday to Monday 13:00–16:00), is repaid by a fine outlook across Monterey Bay.

Between October and March, Pacific Grove is home to tens of thousands of **Monarch butterflies** on their annual migration from Alaska. The butterflies congregate on the trees along Ridge Road, their wings forming blankets of yellow and black. Pacific Grove also makes one end of the **17-mile Drive** (27km), a pay-to-enter marked route through the interior of the peninsula, passing the much-photographed **Lone Cypress Tree** (defying the ocean wind atop a rocky outcrop) and concluding close to Carmel.

Below: *Boats in Monterey's harbour.*

Carmel **

Carmel's 5000 residents are typically well-heeled and very protective of the half-timbered cottages
which characterize their diminutive town. The whimsical architecture stems from a 1920s initia-
tive to sell property in the then
isolated coastal settlement to
moneyed urban Californians with
back-to-nature leanings. Today,
Carmel's centre is dominated by
upmarket art galleries, boutiques and restaurants, though
all conform to the building regulations intended to preserve Carmel's distinctive looks and outlaw such vul-
garisms as traffic lights and fast-food stands.

Above: *The beautiful
Monterey Peninsula's
much-photographed lone
cypress tree.*

The compact town justifies an hour's stroll, which
should conclude at **Carmel beach**, its white sands bor-
dered by cypress trees. Above the beach to the south, is the
striking **Tor House** (tours Friday and Saturday hourly
10:00–15:00). Built with granite boulders hauled on horse-
back from the shore, it is the former residence of poet
Robinson Jeffers whose narrative verses were often inspired
in part by the rugged beauty of the local coast. One of
California's leading literary figures, Jeffers died in 1962 and
the house now holds mementoes of his life and work.

Carmel Mission ***

Just south of the pretty village of Carmel stands the **Carmel
Mission**, the aesthetic appeal of its Moorish-domed stone
church heightened considerably by the vivid greenery of
the splendidly maintained grounds. Founded in 1771, this
was the second in the chain of 21 missions and became
the headquarters of Junipero Serra, the leader of Spain's
Sacred Expedition through California, and the baptismal
site of 4000 Native Americans. With maps and assorted
artefacts, the mission's museum outlines the story of the
Californian missions, and Serra's spartan living quarters
and library have been effectively restored. Open
Monday–Saturday 09:00–17:00; Sunday 10:30–17:00.

CARMEL'S BACH FESTIVAL

For three weeks from mid-July,
Carmel's Bach Festival celebrates the music of the
German composer, and classical music in general, with outdoor concerts and assorted
events around the town, culmi-
nating in a candle-lit evening
recital at **Carmel Mission**.
Tickets sell out extremely
quickly; tel: (831) 624-2046.

Above: *A daring rodeo performance at a Californian summer festival.*

Point Lobos State Reserve ★★

Situated 3 miles (5km) south of Carmel, Point Lobos State Reserve offers protection to a multitude of coastal creatures, notably the Californian sea lion – whose persistent barks fill the air – and the endangered Californian sea otter. Trails weave around the reserve's wind- and wave-sculptured coves, caves and craggy headlands and, between December and May, luck may bring views of California gray whales migrating from Alaska to the warmer waters off Baja California (Mexico).

Salinas ★

A farming town well off the tourist track, though only 11 miles (18km) inland from Monterey, Salinas makes the most of its associations with **John Steinbeck**, the author of many celebrated books including *Cannery Row* (see p. 74), *East of Eden* and *The Grapes of Wrath*. He also won the 1962 Nobel Prize for Literature. Steinbeck was born in Salinas in 1902 at 132 Central Avenue, now a gourmet lunch restaurant (though offering short tours on weekday lunchtimes). The **National Steinbeck Center** (371 Main Street; open daily 10:00–17:00) is the best place to learn about Steinbeck, his work, and his local links through interactive exhibits and displays. A **Steinbeck Festival** takes place each August in Salinas, which is also the venue of the **California Rodeo**, bronco bucking and other cowboy skills demonstrated over two weeks of June.

Big Sur ★★

Big Sur is a 60-mile (97km) strip of untamed coast which begins some 20 miles (32km) south of Carmel. The **Santa Lucia Mountains** here meet the Pacific Ocean in a succession of dramatic bluffs and headlands, while the twisting and weaving Highway 1 makes frequent crossings of narrow bridges spanning deep gorges. As fog glides through the canyons and waves send torrents of spray skywards, the outlook becomes a memorable one. Human settlement is minimal, though the village of Big Sur offers food and supplies, and the small **Henry Miller Memorial Library** (in summer Wednesday–Monday 11:00–18:00; otherwise Thursday–Sunday 11:00–18:00) remembers the controversial author of *Tropic of Cancer* who lived here for 17 years from 1944.

While many are content to do no more than drive through Big Sur, the area can be explored more closely by swimming, hiking and horse riding in the area's two major state parks: **Andrew Molera** and **Pfeiffer Big Sur**, both accessible from Highway 1.

HEARST CASTLE AND VICINITY

Hearst Castle is the second-biggest tourist attraction in California and brings people to what might otherwise be a forgotten segment of the Central Coast. Yet, while the monumentally extravagant former home of the mega-rich William Randolph Hearst should be on everybody's itinerary, it would be a mistake to ignore the smaller communities in the vicinity, whose understated charm provides a welcome antidote to the Hearst excesses and do much to illustrate the quiet pace of Californian life away from the big cities.

Hearst Castle ★★★

On a hilltop site high above Highway 1 (follow the signs and park at the visitors' centre at the foot of the hill), Hearst Castle was created from a mish-mash of Italian ceilings, French fireplaces, Persian carpets, Flemish tapestries and scores of other items collected with no consideration for cost or for architectural cohesion by the mind-numbingly wealthy publishing tycoon William Randolph Hearst over a 28-year period from 1919.

Below: *A stop on every tourist's itinerary should be the eclectically-styled Hearst Castle.*

WILLIAM RANDOLPH HEARST

An indulged only child and expelled from Harvard for 'a prank', William Randolph Hearst got his start in publishing the easy way, when his wealthy father gave him the ailing *San Francisco Examiner* in 1887. Hearst's booming headlines and salacious stories boosted sales and he moved to New York, creating a vast publishing empire and helping instigate the US-Spanish War to increase circulation in 1898. With his political ambitions thwarted, Hearst embraced indulgence on a grand scale, creating Hearst Castle and moving around it, according to writer Anita Loos, 'with the stately grace of a circus elephant'.

Hearst, the subject of Orson Welles' film, *Citizen Kane*, was the son of a mining baron and made his millions from a media empire. At one time it included nine magazines and 22 daily newspapers, with which he pioneered the sensationalist style dubbed 'yellow journalism'.

While Hearst excelled at spending money – the castle included 38 bedrooms, a marble-floored pool lined by million-dollar statuary, and the world's largest privately owned zoo – accounting was not his strong point. The Depression ended the tumultuous profits of Hearst's publishing interests and he died in 1951 owing large amounts in tax. In return for a $50-million write off, the Hearst family donated the castle to the state of California in 1957 and it is now administered as a state park.

Only accessible on guided tours, the castle is far too large to cover in full on a single visit and three separate 90-minute explorations are offered. Tour 1 is ideal for first-time visitors, as is a fourth which concentrates on the castle's lavish gardens. Particularly in summer, **tour reservations** should be made at least a day ahead of arrival (tel: 1-800 444-4445 or www.hearstcastle.org).

San Simeon ★

The village of San Simeon grew to provide living quarters for Hearst's retinue of servants and staff and experienced a second spurt of expansion as rows of motels arose to accommodate tourists destined for the castle. One of the few items pre-dating the castle is **Sebastian's General Store**, an amusingly ramshackle symbol of old time consumerism, dating from 1852. Sheltered by San Simeon Point, immediately north, the placid **William Randolph Hearst State Beach**, dominated by a 1000ft-long (305m) fishing pier, is the perfect spot for a picnic lunch and to ponder the fact that much of the surrounding land is still owned by the Hearst family.

Above: *An old school building defies the passing years at San Simeon.*
Opposite: *Hearst Castle's Neptune Pool.*

Cambria ★

Cambria, 5 miles (8km) south of San Simeon, has few reasons to warrant a call, although several interesting arts and crafts shops sit among the souvenir outlets on either side of Highway 1. A leisurely evening stroll along nearby **Moonstone Beach** is as good a way as any to enjoy a Central Coast sunset.

Morro Bay ★

In the tiny community of Morro Bay, 25 miles (40km) south of San Simeon, your attention will unfailingly come to rest on the 576ft-high (202m) **Morro Rock**, a volcanic hunk which is a protected nesting ground for numerous bird species, including the majestic peregrine falcon. The local economy is reliant on the fishing fleet, whose catch is prepared by the seafood eateries grouped along the bayfront. Just south, **Morro Bay State Park** has a worthwhile **Museum of Natural History**, describing the ecological importance of the local wetlands and the sand dunes which form the slender peninsula that shelters the bay. Open daily 10:00–17:00.

A GRACIOUS LADY

While her husband concentrated on his mining business and her son on his media empire, **Phoebe Apperson Hearst**, mother of William Randolph, earned herself affection among Californians for the numerous donations and endowments – totalling $21 million – she made to improve the state's education system. She underwrote the architectural competition for the design of the University of California campus at Berkeley in 1896 and later financed the university's much-lauded archaeological expeditions around the globe.

Above: *Montana de Oro State Park, San Luis Obispo.*

San Luis Obispo ★★

San Luis Obispo, 9 miles (14km) south of Morro Bay at the junction of highways 1 and 101, is among California's least ostentatious but most appealing towns. It grew around a mission, **San Luis Obispo de Tolosa**, founded in 1772 and now sitting in a proud state of preservation in the town centre. Wandering through the echoey rooms and corridors of the mission is entertaining though not particularly informative, given the paucity of original items and historical documentation (open daily 09:00–16:00 or 17:00). A few minutes' walk away, a more comprehensive clutter – Native American artefacts, pioneer family photos, old furnishings and more – records the town's past and fills the **County Historical Museum**, 696 Monterey Street (open Wednesday–Sunday 10:00–16:00). San Luis Obispo is at its best on Thursday evenings when the entire population, it seems, decants to Higuera Street for the **Farmers' Market** – an excuse to snack from outdoor food stalls, listen to impromptu live music and generally have a good time.

Pismo Beach ★

Californians know Pismo Beach, 12 miles (19km) southwest of San Luis Obispo on Highway 1, for one thing only: Pismo clams, claimed to be a more succulent variety than those found elsewhere along the coast. Such is their popularity that the picking of clams is now strictly controlled to preserve stocks. The best time to sample the great crustacean is during October's very well-attended **Pismo Beach Clam Festival**.

Arroyo Grande ★

Californian small towns seldom come better preserved than Arroyo Grande, just off Highway 101 south of Pismo Beach and may be reached directly from San Luis Obispo with Highway 227. It makes a great show of its 20 or so buildings dating from the 1890s to the 1920s. The village's popularity is indicated by the 250,000 people who attend its **Strawberry Festival**, held each Memorial Day Weekend, a fruit-eating extravaganza celebrating the best-loved local crop.

SANTA BARBARA AND THE SANTA YNEZ VALLEY

About 60 miles (97km) south of Hearst Castle, the character of the Central Coast changes dramatically. As the coast turns to face south rather than west, fog-shrouded canyons and wave-lashed bluffs give way to beaches bathed in year-round sunshine. Santa Barbara is by far the largest town in the area and one which combines stunning architecture with an expansive swath of sand. Around Santa Barbara lies evidence of the prehistoric **Chumash** people and the state's major reconstructed mission complex.

NIPOMO DUNES PRESERVE

Immediately south of **Pismo Beach**, alongside the brown pelicans, lest terns and other bird and plant species which enjoy the protection bestowed by state ownership of the 3400-acre (1376ha) expanse of sand dunes known as the **Nipomo Dunes Preserve**, is the buried set of the 1923 Cecil B. DeMille film, **The Ten Commandments**. Excavation of the remains, which include several four-tonne replica Phoenix, began in 1990.

Below: A rooftop view from Santa Barbara's County Courthouse.

Above: *A section of La Purisima Mission State Historic Park.*
Below: *Enjoying the ocean at Santa Barbara.*

Santa Barbara ★★★

Set beneath forested hills and along a seductively curving section of coast, Santa Barbara is characterized by Spanish Colonial (known in California as 'mission-style') architecture. The style dates from Santa Barbara's 1920s rebuilding after a major earthquake and is most successfully expressed by the **County Courthouse**, 1100 Anacapa Street (open Monday–Friday 08:00–16:45; weekends 10:00–16:30). The belltower also offers splendid views across the town's red-tiled rooftops. Within a few strides, the **El Presidio State Historic Park**, 122-129 E Cañon Perdido, spills across several streets holding restored segments of the town's Spanish *presidio*, or fortress, of the 1780s (open daily 10:00–16:30). The **Historical Museum**, 136 E De la Guerra Street, carries a more general account of local history (open Tuesday– Saturday 10:00–17:00; Sunday 12:00–17:00).

Ironically, amid the profusion of Spanish architecture, the **Mission Santa Barbara**, E Los Olivos Street (open daily 09:30–17:00), has a neoclassical look resulting from an 1820 remodelling. Nonetheless, the mission is among the best preserved in the state and enjoys a picturesque setting overlooking the town.

CHUMASH PAINTED CAVE

Reached by a side road off Highway 154 between Santa Barbara and Santa Ynez, the Chumash Painted Cave holds a rock painting believed to date from AD1000 and to have been of cultural importance to the **Chumash people**, Native Americans indigenous to the area. Some 8–10,000 Chumash, also skilled in pottery, basketry and boat building, are thought to have existed at the time of European contact but, largely through lack of resistance to European-borne diseases, virtually all had died by 1910.

Left: *The reconstructed soldiers' barracks at La Purisima Mission State Historic Park.*

Santa Barbara's inviting beach is reason enough for sticking around, though be sure to allocate a few hours to the **Botanic Garden**, 1212 Mission Canyon Road, which holds 5 miles (8km) of pathways and cloaks the walls of a canyon with a thousand different species of native Californian vegetation (open daily 09:00–17:00; reduced hours in winter).

Santa Ynez ★

Situated 30 miles (48km) northwest from Santa Barbara on the steep San Marcos Pass (Highway 154), Santa Ynez's **Valley Historical Society Museum**, 3569 Sagunto Street, helps put the past into perspective, being particularly informative on the Chumash people who inhabited the region prior to European settlement (open Wednesday–Sunday 12:00–16:00). A bigger local draw, though, are wineries. **Buttonwood Farm** and the **Brander Vineyard** are two of many offering free tours and tastings, and can be found just north of Santa Ynez in Los Olivos.

La Purisima Mission State Historic Park ★★

About 23 miles (37km) west of Santa Ynez, La Purisima Mission State Historic Park (open daily 09:00–17:00) is a major reconstruction of **Mission La Purisima Concepcion**, founded in 1771. The buildings, raised since the 1930s using traditional methods, tools and materials, include a soldiers' barracks, soap factory and tannery, and suggest the reality of early 1800s mission life in California.

SOLVANG

Founded by Danish-Americans in the 1910s, Solvang, directly west of Santa Ynez, has evolved into a tacky if mildly amusing pastiche of a **Danish** town, complete with wooden storks and over-priced 'Danish' pastries offered by numerous bakeries. On the eastern periphery, Mission **Santa Ines** was founded in 1804 with the purpose of converting the Chumash to Christianity. The mission now holds a few objects of minor historical note and boasts some lush and lovely gardens.

BEST TIMES TO VISIT

Heavy rainfall afflicts much of the Central Coast between **November** and **March**, and even when the rain subsides, persistently overcast skies and fogs obscure the most spectacular views. Milder conditions prevail between **May** and **September**, much the best time to visit. Santa Barbara and surrounds are welcoming year-round with mild winters and very warm summers tempered by fresh ocean breezes.

GETTING THERE

Although all the major settlements have regional **airports** with good domestic connections, the Central Coast is best reached and toured by **car**, its northern and southern extremities being within a two-hour drive of San Francisco and Los Angeles respectively. Infrequent Greyhound **buses** link Santa Cruz, Monterey, San Luis Obispo and Santa Barbara but do not take the scenic coastal route. Even less frequent Amtrak **trains** call at Salinas, San Luis Obispo and Santa Barbara.

GETTING AROUND

A **car** is the best way to tour the Central Coast. Though narrow and slow by Californian standards, Highway 1 (occasionally combined with Highway 101) runs the length of the coast.

Local **buses**, reliable during weekdays but infrequent at weekends, serve the communities of the Monterey Peninsula and Salinas and (in summer) Big Sur village.

WHERE TO STAY

Santa Cruz and the Monterey Peninsula
LUXURY
Highlands Inn, off Highway 1 immediately south of Carmel, tel: (831) 620-1234, fax: 626-1574. The pick of the tastefully furnished rooms boast cozy fireplaces and wonderful ocean-view balconies.
MID-RANGE
Babbling Brook Inn, 1025 Laurel Street, Santa Cruz, tel: (831) 427-2437, fax: 427-2457. In keeping with the European rural theme, each of the 12 bed-and-breakfast rooms in this inviting 1909 building, is named after a French painter – an inspiring environment.
The Monterey Hotel, 406 Alvarado Street, Monterey, tel: toll free 1-800 727-0960, (831) fax: 373-2899. Competitively priced and centrally located, an ideal choice for exploring the heart of Monterey.
BUDGET
Capri Motel, 337 Riverside Avenue, Santa Cruz, tel: (831) 426-4611. Probably the least costly of Santa Cruz's numerous plain but acceptable motels.

Hearst Castle and Vicinity
LUXURY
San Luis Bay Inn Resort, Avila Beach, tel: (805) 595-2333, fax: (805) 549-2917. The grounds include an 18-hole golf course and the suites come equipped with hot tubs.
MID-RANGE
Madonna Inn, 100 Madonna Way, San Luis Obispo, tel: (805) 543-3000, fax: 543-1800. As much a tourist attraction as a hotel with 109 individually themed, comfortable rooms and a host of eccentric features.
BUDGET
Peach Tree Inn, 2001 Monterey Street, San Luis Obispo, tel: (805) 543-3170, fax: (805) 543-7673. The best of scores of motels on the route into town, with simple rooms and a pleasant, relaxing setting.

Santa Barbara and the Santa Ynez Valley
LUXURY
El Encanto, 1900 Lasuen Road, Santa Barbara, tel: (805) 568-1357, fax: 687-0943. Gorgeous, well-equipped cottages secreted in the forested foothills above the town.
MID-RANGE
Casa Del Mar, 18 Bath Street, Santa Barbara, tel: (805) 963-4418, fax: 966-4240. Comfortable rooms set around a Mediterranean-style courtyard with a pool.
Harbor View Inn, 28 W Cabrillo Drive, Santa Barbara,

tel: (805) 963-0780, fax: 963-7967. Classy but affordable accommodation, and overlooking the ocean.

BUDGET
Banana Bungalow, 134 Chapala Street, Santa Barbara, tel: (805) 963-0154. Lively hostal, perfect for the budget traveller.

WHERE TO EAT

Santa Cruz and the Monterey Peninsula
MID-RANGE
Café Brasil, 1410 Mission Boulevard, tel: (831) 429-1855. Tasty assortment of Brazilian-influenced dishes, with creative vegetarian choices and delicious fruit juices.
Nepenthe, off Highway 1, 28 miles (45km) south of Carmel, tel: (831) 667-2345. Idyllic setting overlooking the Big Sur coastline with an informal mood and general range of tasty California fare.
Corner View, 1140 Chorro Street, San Luis Obispo, tel: (805) 546-8444. Wide-ranging menu of American favourites such as meatloaf and much more besides.
BUDGET
Jitlada, 107 Leonard Street, Santa Cruz, tel: (831) 420-1688. Great value Thai food.
Linnaea's Café, 1110 Garden Street, San Luis Obispo, tel: (805) 541-5888. Popular with locals for 20 years thanks to its ever-changing, always health-conscious offerings.

Hearst Castle and Vicinity
LUXURY
Windows on the Water, 699 Embarcadero, Morro Bay, tel: (850) 772-0677. Wonderful ocean views are matched by the spectacular, predominantly seafood, dishes.
MID-RANGE
The Apple Farm, 2015 Monterey Street, San Luis Obispo, tel: (805) 544-6100. Deservedly popular for its tasty rural American dishes.
BUDGET
Big Sky Café, 1121 Broad Street, San Luis Obispo, tel: (805) 545-5401. Scrumptious vegetarian breakfast and lunches, and equally good, if pricier, dinners.
Downtown Brewing Company, 1119 Garden Street, San Luis Obispo, tel: (805) 543-1843. Steaks, burgers and sandwiches feature on a menu enlivened by its own-brewed beers.

Santa Barbara and the Santa Ynez Valley
LUXURY
Stella Mare's, 50 Los Patos Way, Santa Barbara, tel: (805) 969-6705. Outstanding, predominantly French-influenced cuisine. Victorian building overlooking a bird sanctuary.
MID-RANGE
Art & Letters Café, 7 East Anapamu Street, Santa Barbara, tel: (805) 730-1463. Diverse fare with a seafood accent, elegantly served amid artworks.

Palace Grill, 8 E Cota Street, Santa Barbara, tel: (805) 963-5000. Stylish and fiery cajun and creole fare.
Your Place, 22 N Milpas Street, Santa Barbara, tel: (805) 966-5151. Thai eatery, menu includes numerous vegetarian options.
BUDGET
Natural Café, 508 State Street, Santa Barbara, tel: (805) 962-9494. Very healthy and diverse vegetarian meals and snacks.

TOURS AND EXCURSIONS

The Channel Islands National Park is a string of desert islands off the Central Coast protected as a wildlife preserve, that can be visited by boat from Santa Barbara and from Ventura, 35 miles (56km) south of Santa Barbara. Excellent hiking, fishing, and skin-diving through shipwrecks is on offer. For details, contact **Island Packers**, tel: (805) 642-1393.

USEFUL CONTACTS

Santa Cruz County Conference and Visitors Council, 1211 Ocean Street, Santa Cruz, tel: (831) 425-1234 or (800) 833-3494, www.santacruzca.org
Monterey Chamber of Commerce, www.mpcc.com
Hearst Castle, tel: 1-800 444-4445, www.hearstcastle.org
Santa Barbara Conference and Visitors Bureau, 1601 Anacapa Street, Santa Barbara, tel: (805) 966-9222 or (800) 549-5133, www.santabarbaraca.com

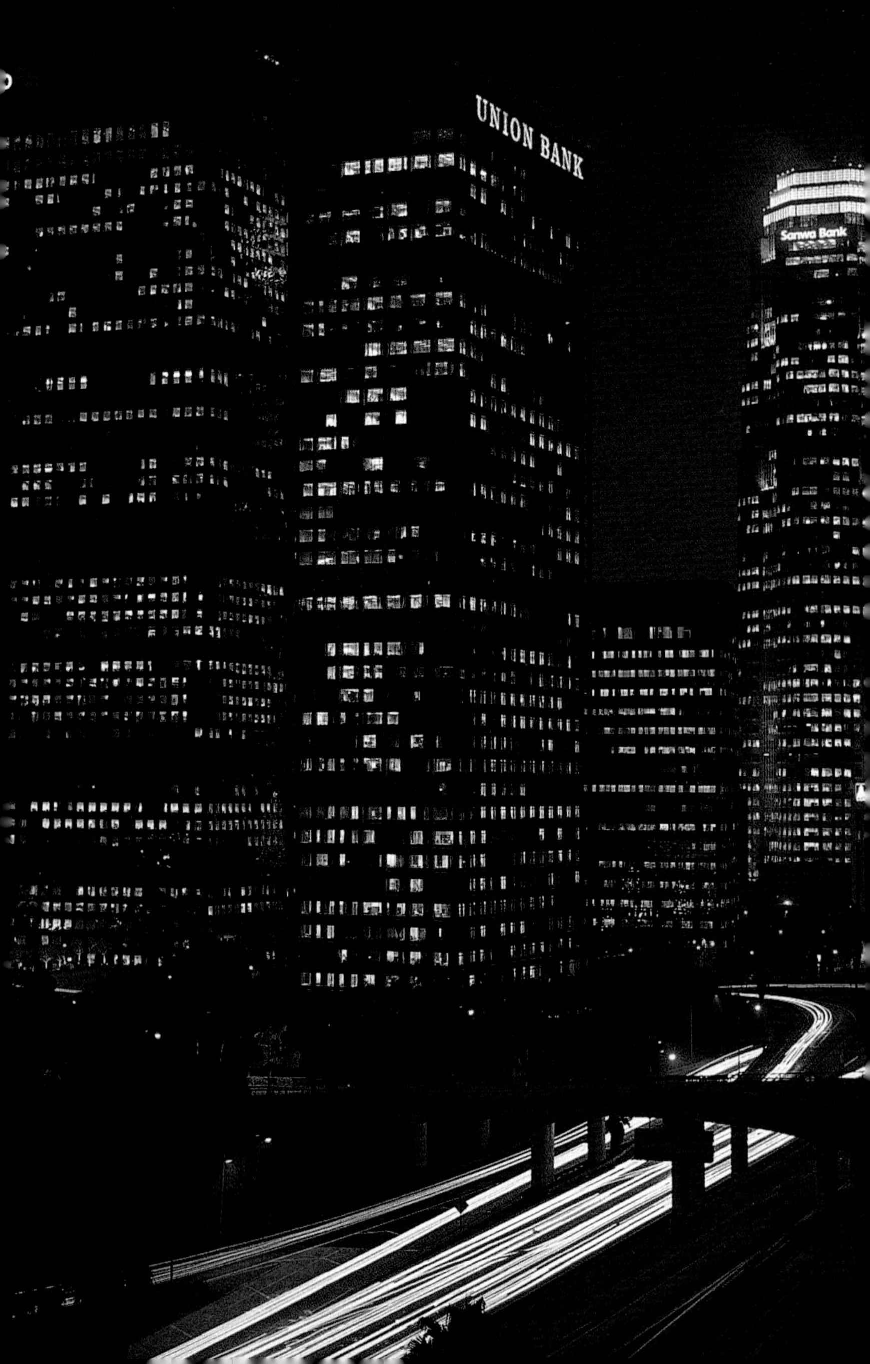
UNION BANK
Sanwa Bank

6
Los Angeles

Able to thrill, terrify and amuse all at the same time, Los Angeles is a city like no other and has been defying logic since its earliest days. Now the second-biggest city in the USA, Los Angeles has no natural water supply and survives despite being regularly rocked by earthquakes. Los Angeles has enough architectural landmarks, world-class museums, beautiful beaches and million-dollar homes to occupy the most demanding visitor. The city has also regained some self-esteem after a troubled 1990s when the Rodney King riots and the OJ Simpson affair highlighted the stresses within its social fabric.

This immense metropolis fills a 4000-sq-mile (10,363km²) basin encompassing 88 separate cities, their boundaries barely discernible in an urban sprawl of shopping malls, petrol stations and fast-food outlets. The small section that the rest of the world calls Los Angeles – and which is safe for visitors – is a slender 15-mile (24km) slice between **Downtown** and the coast. This includes **Hollywood**, **Beverly Hills**, **Santa Monica**, **Venice Beach** and **Malibu**. Within easy reach by car are **Disneyland**®, several other theme parks, plus outlying attractions such as **Glendale's Forest Lawn Cemetery** and **Pasadena**.

Many areas can be explored on foot but a car is essential to travel between them. Local bus travel is slow. No-go areas – such as South Central LA – tend to be far from the main track but the side streets of Hollywood and Venice Beach must be treated with caution.

DON'T MISS

*** **Disneyland**®: the mother of all theme parks.
*** **Venice Beach:** the Boardwalk sees a parade of free-and-easy LA lifestyles.
*** **Museum of Tolerance:** powerful examinations of human bigotry.
** **Griffith Park:** acres of walks, hikes and horse-rides in the heart of the city.
*** **The Getty Centre:** Fantastic art in an even more fantastic setting.
* **Forest Lawn Cemetery:** celebrity tombs and ostentatious art and architecture.

Opposite: *Los Angeles.*

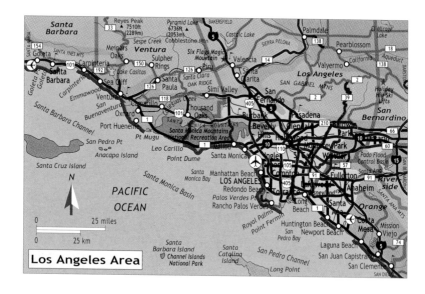

Los Angeles Area

DOWNTOWN

Though its bustling streets can seem intimidating and the high-rise offices and underground shopping complexes appear entirely soulless, Downtown Los Angeles does have some points – a smattering of architectural landmarks, a major contemporary art showplace, and the well-preserved birthplace of the city – in its favour and all these sights are within walking distance of one another.

El Pueblo de Los Angeles State Historic Park ★★

The first 44 ethnically mixed Angelenos who arrived in 1781 settled on the northeastern edge of what is now Downtown, in an area now corralled by El Pueblo de Los Angeles State Historic Park. The park retains a few 1800s adobe buildings, including the 1818 **Avila Abode**, the city's oldest house, and is dominated by the pseudo-Mexican market along **Olvera Street**. Created in the 1930s as a tourist attraction, Olvera Street has low-key charm and dozens of low-cost spots to sample Mexican food. The park's full background is explained inside the **Visitor Information Center**, 622 N Main Street (open

Monday–Friday 10:00–15:00, Saturday 10:00–16:30), and on free guided tours from 130 Paseo de la Plaza, tel: (213) 628-1274.

Union Station ★★★
Archways, tiled roofs and a belltower are among the pleasing features of Union Station, 800 N Alameda Street. To savour the atmosphere, stride across the marble floor into the echoey waiting room and fall into a bench seat deep enough to drown in.

City Hall ★
City Hall, 200 N Spring Street, was the highest building in Los Angeles on completion in 1928 and remained so until the 1950s. The ascent to the 27th-floor observation level offers a chance to take in the Art Deco fittings before enjoying a view across the city (smog-permitting).

Grand Central Market ★★
Broadway is the main artery of Downtown and on it stands the bustling Grand Central Market, 317 S Broadway. The perfect antidote to Los Angeles's shopping malls, Grand Central Market has been dispensing meat, fruit, vegetables and much more, from open stalls in a noisy indoor setting since the 1930s. Open Monday–Sunday 09:00–18:00.

Museum of Contemporary Art ★★★
Opened in the 1980s and designed by noted architect Arata Isozaki, the Museum of Contemporary Art was intended to put LA on the international art world map and undermine New York's modern art supremacy. To this end, MOCA holds pieces by the major names from the 1940s onwards and is particularly well-stocked with the leading names of Abstract Expressionism and

DOWNTOWN Other than the shade they might proffer on a sunny day, the high-rise towers of Downtown's **Financial District** have little appeal. Sprouting impudently among them, however, is Frank Gehry's Disney Concert Hall, 111 S Grand Avenue, with its undulating curves giving the impression of huge metallic sails and with hardly a rectangle to be found. The building, planned since the 1980s, opened in November 2003 having cost $274 million.

Below: *The instantly recognizable landmark.*

Pop Art; Jasper John's *Map* is just one notable item. Equally stimulating, however, are the frequent temporary exhibitions of international repute. Open Wednesday–Friday 11:00–17:00; Thursday until 20:00; weekends 11:00–18:00.

HOLLYWOOD

Few neighbourhoods have the cultural resonance or the tourist appeal of Hollywood, home of the US film industry from the 1910s and a byword for glamour, wealth and opportunity ever since. Yet while it does have movie landmarks in abundance, today's Hollywood is an often tawdry and sometimes dangerous place (especially so at night); visitors should stick to the safe areas.

Chinese Theatre ★

Opened by impresario Sid Grauman in 1927, the Chinese Theatre, 6925 Hollywood Boulevard, quickly became a Hollywood landmark by dint of its star-attended movie premiers and by the (mostly) hand- and foot-prints made by celebrities in concrete on its forecourt. The practice began with Norma Talmadge in 1928 and continues into the present: actual prints are shown on a rotating schedule.

Hollywood Bowl ★★

Occupying a 50-acre (20ha) natural amphitheatre in the hills immediately above Hollywood, is the 20,000-seat Hollywood Bowl, 2301 Highland Avenue. It famously hosted the Beatles in 1964 but is adored by Angelenos for the summer concerts given by the LA Philharmonic. An on-site museum reveals the background of the Bowl and its Frank Lloyd Wright-designed features. Open Tuesday–Friday 10:00–17:00; until later in summer and weekends.

Hollywood Forever Cemetery ★★

Los Angeles cemeteries are very popular with tourists who come to see the tombstones of legendary screen stars. Adjoining **Paramount Studios** (whose much-photographed gates abut Melrose Avenue), is the Hollywood Forever Cemetery, 6000 Santa Monica Boulevard (open daily 08:00–17:00 or dusk). It has an impressive roll-call of major names – among them Cecil B. DeMille, Tyrone Power and Douglas Fairbanks Jnr – but the most visited section is the cathedral mausoleum where Crypt 1205 holds the remains of handsome, silent-screen lover Rudolph Valentino, laid to rest here in 1926.

Griffith Park ★★

Encompassing picnic areas, a zoo, a bird sanctuary, golf courses, tennis courts and 52 separate hiking trails as it rises from the edge of Hollywood into the Santa Monica Mountains, the 3761 acres (1522ha) of Griffith Park come as a big surprise in car-dependent LA.

The park's best-known feature, seen in movies from *Rebel Without a Cause* to *Barton Fink*, is the copper-domed **Griffith Park Observatory**, site of plane-tarium and laserium shows. On clear nights it offers the opportunity to scan

HOLLYHOCK HOUSE

Among the most accessible of the many notable examples of modern architecture scattered throughout Hollywood is the Hollyhock House, in Barnsdall Park close to the junction of Hollywood Boulevard and Vermont Avenue.

Designed by **Frank Lloyd Wright** for oil heiress Aline Barnsdall in the 1920s, the house makes free use of Mayan motifs and is partly patterned on a hollyhock. Tours, tel: (323) 644-6269.

Below: *Hollywood Chinese Theatre, where the movie stars leave their mark.*

the heavens with a 10-inch (254mm) telescope. From the observatory, a hiking trail leads to the 1600ft (488m) summit of Mount Hollywood. Safe during the day, Griffith Park should be avoided at night.

Autry Museum of Western Heritage ★★★

Situated on the northeastern corner of Griffith Park, best reached by car from the junction of Golden State and Ventura freeways. The Gene Autry Western Heritage Museum provides an impressive account, over two copiously stocked floors, of the settlement of the American West and the rise of the Hollywood Western. Open Tuesday–Sunday 10:00–17:00; Thursday until 20:00.

BEVERLY HILLS, WEST LA AND WILSHIRE BOULEVARD

Beverly Hills is synonymous with money and celebrity status even though there are wealthy, star-studded neighbourhoods across much of the rest of West LA. The aura of affluence can also be felt along Wilshire Boulevard, which scythes through West LA on its 15 miles (24km) route between Downtown and the coast and holds many of the area's major points of interest.

Los Angeles County Museum of Art ★★

Be it German Expressionism, pre-Columbian Mexican art or Chinese watercolours, the collections of the Los Angeles County Museum of Art, 5909 Wilshire Boulevard,

are exhaustive and exhausting and will need at least a day to comprehensively view. Sensible visitors pace themselves, choosing sections of personal interest and concentrating on them. Be sure, however, to save time for the **Pavilion for Japanese Art**, an architecturally innovative 1988 addition within which is an extraordinary collection of Edo-period paintings, plus many extremely fine netsuke. Open Monday, Tuesday, Thursday 12:00–20:00; Friday 12:00–21:00; weekends 11:00–20:00.

La Brea Tar Pits ★★

The naming of La Brea Avenue with the Spanish word for tar was no accident: natural tar deposits lie beneath its junction with Wilshire Boulevard and in prehistoric times many creatures met their ends in the sticky, thick substance. Since excavation began in 1906, over a million fossilized bones have been extracted from the La Brea Tar Pits, 5801 Wilshire Boulevard (open Tuesday–Sunday 09:30–17:00). The adjoining, small **George C. Page Museum** (same hours as La Brea Tar Pits) chronicles the finds and the continuing archaeological work.

Above: *A typically well-scrubbed street in Beverly Hills.*
Opposite: *Inside or out, viewing is easy at this Los Angeles gallery.*

Westwood Village and UCLA ★

One of the few parts of LA designed for pedestrians, Westwood Village, just west of Beverly Hills, was laid out in the 1920s as a Mediterranean-style shopping plaza. Nowadays the shops – and an amazing number of cinemas – are visited mostly by students spilling over from the adjacent **University of California** at Los Angeles (UCLA). A stroll through a few of the campus's 400 acres (162ha) leads to the attractive grouping of brick-built Italianate structures at its heart and several minor museums.

Museum of Tolerance ★★★

Interactive computers and inventive audio-visual installations explore racism and prejudice in the USA, and a substantial area is devoted to documenting Nazism and the holocaust. The Museum of Tolerance, 9760 W Pico Boulevard, is a provocative and very challenging place. Even the most liberal visitors are likely to find their attitudes under scrutiny. Open Monday–Thursday 10:00–18:30, Friday 10:00–13:00, Sunday 11:00–19:30.

FARMERS' MARKET

Farmers' Market, junction of Fairfax Avenue and Third Street in West LA, began during the Depression as a place where growers could sell directly to customers. Such was its success that Farmers' Market is a city landmark with fresh fruit and vegetables and many places to eat.

Above: *Californian beach boys about to hit the surf.*

Armand Hammer Museum of Art & Culture Center ★★

The late oil-magnate Armand Hammer spent some of his incredible wealth on the art collection now displayed at 10899 Wilshire Boulevard. While many major names are represented, the most satisfying inclusions are the lithographs of 19th-century French caricaturist **Honoré Daumier**. More famous – though somewhat anti-climatic – is the **Codex Hammer**: pages from the notebooks of Leonardo da Vinci, which Hammer purchased and, in keeping with previous owners, re-named after himself. Open Tuesday–Saturday 11:00–19:00, Thursday until 21:00, Sunday 11:00–17:00.

COASTAL LOS ANGELES

Compared to the rest of the city, coastal Los Angeles can be, literally, a breath of fresh air. Cooled by smog-removing ocean breezes and set beside an almost unbroken 15-mile (24km) line of sunkissed sands, the city's coastal communities include cosmopolitan Santa Monica, frenzied Venice Beach, and the rich and exclusive Malibu. Malibu's wealth is confirmed by the staggering hoard of the J. Paul Getty Museum.

Below: *Venice Beach's Muscle Beach.*

Santa Monica ★★

Santa Monica borders 3 miles (5km) of sandy beach and a 1990s revitalization which saw the appearance of new high-class hotels and the development of the effervescent **Third Street Promenade**, a pedestrianized strip between Broadway and Wilshire Boulevard lined by sidewalk cafés and restaurants.

Longer established is the 1908 **Santa Monica Pier**, with an ageing carousel (seen in the film *The Sting*) at one end and fine views across the beach – beloved of surfers and sunbathers – at the other. Santa Monica's past is well documented by the entertaining displays of the **California Heritage Museum**, 2612 Main Street. Open Wednesday–Sunday 11:00–16:00.

Venice Beach ★★★

Fire-eaters, escapologists and mime artists mingle among the roller bladers, joggers and bemused onlookers who are all part of the chaos of **Venice Beach** and its beachside Boardwalk, directly south of Santa Monica. Beyond the Boardwalk, which also holds **Muscle Beach**, an open-air gym for bodybuilders unconcerned about sunburn, Venice has little to see. Curiously, though, it was founded by a tobacco baron with a dream of re-creating the town's Italian namesake; he even built 16 miles (26km) of canals, long-since filled in.

The Getty Center ★★★

Before his death in 1976, the ultra-rich oil baron, J.Paul Getty, spent a small part of his vast fortune on Roman and Greek antiquities and set in motion the chain of events that would see this awe-inspiring museum built in the hills overlooking LA and the coast. Completed in 1998 at a cost of a billion dollars, the centre houses a world-class stash of European art from the Renaissance to the Post Impressionists in a serious of pavilions linked by plazas and terraces, all with breathtaking views. Entry to this extraordinary museum is free although parking (approach from I-405) is not and a space should be reserved, tel: (310) 440-7300. Open Tuesday–Thursday and Sunday 10:00–18:00; Friday and Saturday 10:00–21:00. Getty's former home, a replica Pompeiian villa sited above Malibu displays the Greek and Roman treasures.

WILL ROGERS STATE PARK

In Pacific Palisades, directly north of Santa Monica, Will Rogers State Park, 14253 Sunset Boulevard, preserves the home of Will Rogers – the dryly witty 'Cowboy philosopher' much loved by the American public before being killed in a plane crash in 1935. Stuffed with Navajo rugs, steer skulls, six-shooters and lassos, the ranch-style house could be a set from a Hollywood Western. The grounds are laced with walking and hiking trails.

Left: *The classical extravagance of J. Paul Getty's pseudo-Roman villa – now a museum.*

PALOS VERDES AND WAYFARER'S CHAPEL

Pacific Coast Highway (PCH), which links the coastal towns, turns inland at Palos Verdes peninsula, which marks LA's southwest extremity. Palos Verdes Drive, meanwhile, leaves PCH to climb around the peninsula's clifftops, revealing stunning ocean views and Wayfarer's Chapel, number 5755. Designed by Frank Lloyd Wright's son, Lloyd, it is dedicated to Swedish mystic **Emmanual Swedenborg**.

Malibu ★

Malibu's opulent reputation stems from 1926 and 'the colony', an enclave of seclusion-seeking screen stars. Today's Malibu residents have only their ability to afford an astronomically priced home in common. Average-income visitors can at least get a Malibu tan: the town sits at the centre of a string of expansive beaches, busy only at weekends.

THE VALLEYS

The neatly patterned suburbia that fills the **San Gabriel** and **San Fernando** valleys, stretching north from Downtown, gets the worse of LA's summer smog and searing heat, and largely deserves its parochial image. The valleys, however, do hold two worthwhile targets: the high-kitsch **Forest Lawn Cemetery** in Glendale and the charming city of **Pasadena**. The valley's film studios, in North Hollywood and Burbank, are described on pages 98-9.

Forest Lawn Cemetery ★★★

Described by its founder as 'the greenest, most enchanting park you ever saw in your life' and by comedian Lenny Bruce as 'Disneyland® for the dead', Glendale's Forest Lawn Cemetery, 1712 S Glendale Avenue, attracts a million tourists a year. They come partly for its celebrity graves – Walt Disney, Errol Flynn, WC Fields, Clark Gable and Jean Harlow are among the showbiz notables buried here – but also for its grandiose replica art and statuary (open daily 08:00–18:00).

The **Great Mausoleum** holds a stained glass re-working of Da Vinci's *The Last Supper* and Michelangelo's *David* is solemnly reproduced in the Court of David. The cemetery's churches include the Church of the Recessional and the Wee Kirk O'the Heather, modelled on originals in 10th-century England and 14th-century Scotland respectively. Some of the tombs conceal surprises, too: such as the one that plays lullabies when visitors unknowingly trigger a trip-wire.

There are several other Forest Lawn Cemeteries in LA; the others have their share of famous names but only the Glendale branch has art of restraint-defying style.

Below: *A young Clark Gable, famous for his role as Rhett Butler in the epic* Gone with the Wind.

Left: *Colourful façades on a Pasadena Street.*

Pasadena ★★

When smog permits, Pasadena is overlooked by the 1800ft-high (549m) **San Gabriel Mountains** and is the only valley community of substantial appeal. The restored 1910s buildings situated along Colorado Boulevard and the mission-style **City Hall**, 100 N Garfield Avenue, with its archways, dome and plush gardens, both repay a few hours lazy exploration. Also worth visiting, is the **Norton Simon Museum**, 411 W Colorado Boulevard, with a fine stock of European art, ranging from **Reubens** to **Picasso**, alongside world-class Asian sculpture (open Wednesday–Monday 12:00–18:00; Thursday until 21:00).

Pasadena also scores highly for its turn-of-the-century residential architecture, with numerous Craftsman-style homes by the influential local firm of Greene and Greene. The Greenes' skills are most vividly expressed by the 1908 **Gamble House**, 4 Westmoreland Place, in which every detail – from the open-air sleeping porches to the rugs and lighting – was designed by the architects and is maintained in its original form (guided tours Thursday–Sunday 12:00–15:00).

Huntington Library, Art Collection and Botanical Gardens ★★★

An exhibition on Greene and Greene can be found just east of Pasadena at the Huntington Library, Art Collection and Botanical Gardens, 1151 Oxford Road. Also competing for attention are **Gainsborough's** *Blue Boy*, a **Guten-**

Above: *Tomorrowland®*
today at Disneyland®.

burg Bible and innumerable other paintings, rare books
and manuscripts. These are all displayed in and around
the former home of 19th-century transport entrepreneur,
Henry E Huntington. Open Tuesday–Friday 12:00–16:30;
weekends 10:30–16:30.

THEME PARKS

With the pacesetting originator, **Disneyland®**, the replicated film sets of **Universal Studios®** and the high-velocity
rollercoasters of **Six Flags Magic Mountain** on its periphery, Los Angeles holds the world's greatest concentration
of theme and amusement parks. Each major park needs a
day to enjoy properly; one steep fee pays for everything
except food, drink, souvenirs and parking.

INFO NUMBERS

Disneyland®:
tel: (714) 781-4565.
Universal Studios® Tour:
tel: (818) 622-3801.
Six Flags Magic Mountain:
tel: (661) 255-4854.
Knott's Berry Farm:
Tel: (714) 220-5200
**Warner Brothers Studios
VIP Tours:**
tel: (818) 972-8687.

Disneyland® ★★★

About 27 miles (43km) southeast of Downtown,
Disneyland® is by far the most popular tourist attraction in
California, averaging 60,000 visitors a day and drawing
over 500 million since its opening in 1955. It's unlikely
that many have left unhappy: the skill of Disneyland® is
not just in its rides and Disney® characters but in subtle
psychology – such as in softening the tedium of queuing –
that causes even would-be cynics to enjoy themselves.

Some of Disneyland's® rides, such as the **Mad Hatters Tea Party** and **Peter Pan's Flight**, seem as old as the park though their popularity with young kids remains undiminished. Others are impressively high-tech: the abuse of a state-of-the-art flight simulator that makes up **Star Tours** means the seat belts really are essential, and the pitch-black roller-coaster of **Space Mountain**® truly is a nerve-jangling experience albeit lasting only three minutes. For more thrills and spills, sample the runaway train of **Big Thunder Mountain Railroad** and the watery descents of **Splash Mountain**®. Meanwhile, Disney's® very clever audio-animatronic characters – robots with sound synchronized to body movement – demonstrate surprising fluency in graveyard humour at the **Haunted Mansion**.

Aim to avoid weekends and public holidays; arrive early to enjoy the most popular rides without a lengthy wait; and check the regularly updated noticeboards to find which rides have the smallest queues. Disney's® newer and neighbouring **Disney's California Adventure**® park is largely underwhelming save for the Tower of Terror, and also requires a separate admission fee.

Universal Studios® ★

Good as Disneyland® is, Universal Studios® (in North Hollywood, follow signs from the Hollywood Freeway) beats it hands down for special-effect rides. Best is **Back To the Future**, a 4-minute trip through 60 million years to the time of the dinosaurs with incredible special effects and endless jolts and bumps. Dinosaurs also appear in

WARNER BROTHERS STUDIO TOURS

By making a reservation (tel: (818) 972-8687) ahead of arrival, you can join the so-called **VIP Tour of Warner Brothers Studios**, 4000 Warner Brothers Boulevard, Burbank. Much less tourist-orientated than Universal Studios®, the two-hour tour reveals a little of the behind-the-scenes activity of a working film studio and allows participants to wander around sets from current TV series. Weekdays only.

Left: *Learning the tricks of the stunt trade at Universal Studios®.*

CATALINA ISLAND FERRIES

Ferries to Catalina Island depart from San Pedro and Long Beach, neighbouring towns 20 miles (32km) south of Downtown LA, and are run by **Catalina Express**, tel: (800) 481-3470, and **Catalina Explorer**, tel: (877) 432-6276. From Newport Beach, the island is served by the **Catalina Passenger Service**, tel: (949) 673-5245.

another tumultuous ride, **Jurassic Park**. **Revenge of the Mummy** also thrills, while fans of the Shrek films should not leave without experiencing the three-dimensional experiences that is the 15-minute **Shrek 4D**.

Six Flags Magic Mountain ★

Anyone who gets dizzy in an elevator should avoid Six Flags Magic Mountain, beside I-5 (Interstate 5) near Valencia, 34 miles (55km) north from Downtown LA, where some of the world highest and fastest roller-coasters do their utmost to scare passengers senseless. **Children's World** has gentler rides for those yet to graduate to the hardcore thrills and spills.

EXCURSIONS

Los Angeles could occupy the most adventurous traveller for weeks but also makes a good base for day-long excursions. The largely undeveloped **Catalina Island** is a two-hour ferry ride away, while a day's drive south along the coast takes in contrasting **Newport Beach** and **Laguna Beach** before reaching Southern California's prettiest mission, just inland at **San Juan Capistrano**.

Catalina Island ★★

Catalina's 2000 inhabitants get around by bicycle or electric moke (car ownership is restricted) and almost all of them live in **Avalon**, a picture-postcard town marked by whimsical architecture and built along a curving bay. Stroll along the seafront from the ferry harbour and you will quickly reach the **Avalon Casino**, holding a museum (open daily 10:00–16:00) outlining the island's history and that of the ballroom, which opened as a casino in the 1920s following Catalina's purchase by William Wrigley Jnr (part of the Wrigley chewing gum dynasty). Wrigley sunk some of the gambling profits into preserving Catalina in its

Below: *The wooden pier at Catalina Island.*

undeveloped form and tours of the **backcountry** – 40,000 acres (16,188ha) of wild, hilly terrain – are recommended, tel: (310) 510-2595.

Newport Beach ★

Poverty appears to have been abolished at Newport Beach, 42 miles (68km) south of Los Angeles, where seemingly everyone lives in a million-dollar home with a yacht docked near-

by. Impressions of major wealth are compounded by the high-price **Fashion Island** shopping centre, beside Highway 1, showing Southern Californian consumerism at its most affluent and soothing. A more enjoyable slice of Newport Beach is found along the 3 mile-long (5km) **Balboa Peninsula**, a lovely swathe of sand. Here too, dare-devil bodysurfers aim to tame **The Wedge**, a small patch of local water legendary for its huge waves.

Above: *Tidily arranged homes and boats at Newport Beach.*

Laguna Beach ★★

Spread across coves and inlets, Laguna Beach, 20 miles (32km) south of Newport Beach, is visually attractive and filled with art galleries and craft shops, a legacy of its 1920s settlement by artists captivated by the natural setting. The **Laguna Beach Art Museum**, 307 Cliff Drive, has a small permanent stock of works by early Laguna Beach artists and regularly exhibits the town's current talents. Open daily 10:00–17:00.

San Juan Capistrano ★★★

About 15 miles (24km) from Laguna Beach, the Mission was founded in 1776 as the seventh in the California chain of 21 Spanish missions. Though much of the original was destroyed by earthquakes in 1812 and 1914, the restoration of the remaining adobe buildings and the immaculately groomed gardens create a sense of charm and historical resonance (open daily 08:30–17:00). Be sure to peek inside the atmospheric **Serra Chapel** – said to be the oldest structure still in use in California.

THE SWALLOWS OF SAN JUAN CAPISTRANO

A popular song of the 1930s gave birth to the legend that the swallows who nest at San Juan Capistrano will return from their annual migration on March 19, **St Joseph's Day**. A festival held at the mission on this date is intended to welcome the swallows back, though their actual return is largely governed by weather conditions. A smaller festival marks their October departure.

Los Angeles at a Glance

Los Angeles can be visited year-round although summers can be very hot and humid, and made less comfortable still by smog. Humidity and smog are least troublesome along the coast. Most rainfall occurs between **October** and **March**.

Los Angeles is a major hub for international and domestic **flights**. The city is also a meeting point for Greyhound **bus** services across the state. Amtrak **train** services arrive several times daily from San Diego with less frequent services from San Francisco and other US cities. All major **road** routes across southern California give good access to the city: I-10 and I-15 from the deserts, I-5 and the coastal Highways 101 and 1 from the north and south, and Highway 14, which links with Highway 395 from the Eastern Sierra.

The city is designed for **car** travel. **Buses** run a comprehensive service but are slow. The **Metro** underground system links Downtown with Long Beach and parts of Hollywood.

Downtown
LUXURY
Biltmore Hotel, 506 S Grand Avenue, tel: (213) 624-1011, fax: (213) 612-1545. Famed for its elegance since 1923.
Westin Bonaventure, 404 S Figueroa Street, tel: (213) 624-1000, fax: (213) 612-4800. Exterior glass-walled lifts. The rooms have every luxury.
MID-RANGE
Figueroa Hotel, 939 S Figueroa Street, tel: (213) 627-8971, fax: (213) 689-0305. Well-equipped, with Spanish-style décor and a pool.
Holiday Inn Downtown, 1020 S Figueroa Street, tel: (213) 748-1291, fax: (213) 748-6028. Part of the dependable nationwide chain.
BUDGET
City Center Motel, 1135 W Seventh Street, tel: (213) 627-2581, fax: (213) 627-8748. Plain but comfortable.

Hollywood
LUXURY
Hollywood Roosevelt, 7000 Hollywood Boulevard, tel: (323) 466-7000, fax: (323) 462-8056. Steeped in movie history.
MID-RANGE
Highland Gardens Hotel, 7047 Franklin Avenue, tel: (213) 850-0536, fax: 850-1712. Dated but very well-located.
Hollywood Metropolitan, 5825 Sunset Boulevard, tel: (323) 962-5800, fax: (323) 466-0646. Well-located, with panoramic views.
BUDGET
Saharan Motor Hotel, 7212 Sunset Boulevard, tel: (323) 874-6700, fax: (323) 876-2625. Serviceable rooms at the area's lowest rates.

Beverly Hills, West LA and Wilshire Boulevard
LUXURY
Beverly Hills Hotel, 9641 Sunset Boulevard, tel: (310) 276-2251, fax: (310) 887-2887. Noted for pampering the great and glamorous.
Hotel Bel Air, 701 Stone Canyon Road, tel: (310) 472-1211, fax: (310) 476-5890. Divine mission-style buildings.
MID-RANGE
Carlyle Inn, 1119 S Robertson Boulevard, tel: (310) 275-4445, fax: (310) 859-0496. Relaxed and appealing; price includes complimentary breakfast buffet and afternoon tea.
Elan Hotel Modern, 8435 Beverly Boulevard, tel: (310) 658-6663, fax: (310) 658-6640. Ultra-stylish boutique hotel.
BUDGET
Los Angeles West Travelodge, 10740 Santa Monica Boulevard, tel: (310) 474-4576, fax: 470-3117. Branch of nationwide chain and reasonably priced.

Coastal LA
LUXURY
Loews Santa Monica Beach Hotel, 1700 Ocean Avenue, Santa Monica, tel (310) 458-6700, fax 458-6761. Right on the ocean with every facility.
MID-RANGE
Shangri-La Hotel, 1301 Ocean Avenue, Santa Monica, tel: (310) 394-2791, fax: (310) 451-3351. Eye-catching Art Deco design inside and out.

Los Angeles at a Glance

BUDGET
Cadillac Hotel, 8 Dudley
Avenue, Venice Beach, tel:
(310) 399-8876, fax: (310)
399-4536. Renovated Art Deco
hotel with beach-side location.
Carmel Hotel-by-the-Sea, 201
Broadway, Santa Monica, tel:
(310) 451-2469, fax: (310)
393-4180. Cozy and convivial.

Where to Eat

Downtown
LUXURY
Water Grill, 544 S Grand
Avenue, tel: (213) 891-0900,
fax: (213) 629-1891. Massively
renowned for its seafood.
MID-RANGE
El Cholo, 1121 S Western
Avenue, tel: (310) 734-2773.
Long-serving Mexican eaterie
– power-packed margaritas.
BUDGET
Original Pantry, 877 S
Figueroa Street, tel: (213) 972-
9279. Long-serving, round-the-
clock meat & potatoes diner.

Hollywood
LUXURY
Campanile, 624 S La Brea
Avenue, tel: (213) 398-1447.
Inventive twists on traditional
Italian cuisine.
MID-RANGE
Toi on Sunset, 7505 Sunset
Boulevard, tel: (323) 874-
8062. Delectable Thai staples
in a funky setting.
BUDGET
Pinks Hot Dog Stand, 711 N
La Brea Avenue, tel: (213)
931-4223. Many believe
these are the world's greatest
hot dogs.

Beverly Hills, West LA
and Wilshire Boulevard
LUXURY
Spago, 176 N Canon Drive,
tel: (310) 385-0880, fax: (310)
385-9690. Probably the city's
most famous restaurant,
opened by a celebrity chef
and feeding LA's famous.
MID-RANGE
California Pizza Kitchen, 207
S Beverly Drive, Beverly Hills,
tel: (310) 275-1101. Quality
chain offering delicious pizzas
and huge fresh salads.
BUDGET
Nate'n Al's, 414 N Beverly
Drive, Beverly Hills, tel: (310)
274-0101. Pricier than the
average coffee shop but a
bargain for the ritzy setting.

Coastal LA
LUXURY
Chinois on Main, 2709 Main
Street, Santa Monica, tel: (310)
392-9025. Creations that have
garnered endless acclaim.
MID-RANGE
Inn of the Seventh Ray,
128 Old Tapanga Road, near
Malibu, tel: (310) 455-1311.
Mostly vegetarian food.

Shopping

You will find almost anything
you're looking for at **Beverly**

Center, corner of Beverly and
La Cienega boulevards, West
LA and the **Glendale Galleria**,
Central Avenue and Wilson
Street, Glendale. Offbeat and
entertaining shops line
Melrose Avenue, West LA.

Tours and Excursions

Free walking tours, **Los
Angeles Conservancy**, tel:
(213) 623-2489. Bus tours are
operated by **Grayline**, tel:
1-800 828-6699, and
Starline, tel: 1-800 959-3131.

Useful Contacts

**Los Angeles Visitor Infor-
mation Center**, 685 S Figueroa
Street, Downtown, tel: (213)
689-8822, www.lacvb.com
Hollywood Visitor Center,
The Janes House, 6541
Hollywood Boulevard,
tel: (323) 467-6412.
Beverly Hills Visitors Bureau,
239 S Beverly Drive, tel: toll
free 1-800 345-2210,
www.beverlyhillsbehere.com
Santa Monica Visitor Center,
1400 Ocean Avenue, tel:
(310) 393-7593, www.santa
monica.com
Pasadena Visitors' Bureau,
171 South Los Robles
Avenue, tel: 1-800 307-7977,
www.pasadenacal.com

LOS ANGELES	J	F	M	A	M	J	J	A	S	O	N	D
AVERAGE TEMP. °C	13	13	14	15	17	18	20	20	20	18	16	14
AVERAGE TEMP. °F	55	55	57	59	63	64	68	68	68	64	61	57
DAYS OF RAINFALL	6	6	6	4	2	1	0	0	1	2	3	6
RAINFALL mm	76	76	51	38	16	8	0	0	4	22	51	81
RAINFALL in	3	3	2	1.5	0.6	0.3	0	0	0.2	1	2	3

7
San Diego
and Surrounds

San Diego is California's most climatically blessed coastal city, with soft ocean breezes keeping the air fresh and free of humidity. Year-round daytime temperatures hover invitingly around 70°F (21°C). The weather, combined with 70 miles (113km) of sandy beach stretching south from the city to the US-Mexico border, and major tourist attractions such as **Sea World**® and **San Diego Zoo**, make the city one of the USA's most popular holiday destinations, earning about $5 billion in visitor revenue annually.

Nonetheless, you can easily spend time in San Diego and never meet a tourist. San Diego is a desirable place to live as well as an agreeable one to visit, its personable and contrasting districts – from the rejuvenated **Downtown** to the hedonistic **Mission Beach** – enjoyed by San Diegans as much as out-of-towners. Affluent and conservative with a strong military presence, San Diego is also a city that radiates health and vitality. Participant sports are pursued with passion, and the city even has a museum dedicated to its sporting prowess.

San Diego is the seventh-largest city in the USA but has little of the sprawl characteristic of Los Angeles. On San Diego's fringes, the urban trappings subside quickly. Even north along the coast, where some of the state's most expensive ocean-view homes stand, a relaxed and friendly small town mood pervades. Heading inland, the roads narrow and the population thins, and forested mountain foothills are only a 90-minute drive away.

Don't Miss

*** San Diego Zoo: for bar-less cages and re-created habitats, few zoos do it better.
*** Balboa Park Museums: set amid Spanish architecture across a huge park.
*** La Jolla: where the coastline, buildings and people look too beautiful to be true.
** Old Town San Diego: buildings from San Diego's formative days.
* Hotel Del Coronado: an architecturally expressive Victorian hotel.

Opposite: *Another perfect day in San Diego.*

SAN DIEGO MISSION

San Diego claims to be the birthplace of European California, being the site of its first Spanish mission. It was founded in 1769 on a hillside site overlooking today's Old Town San Diego. Due to the original location's lack of a water supply and exposure to Native American attack, the mission was moved after four years to a then remote site at 10818 San Diego Mission Road. Still functioning as a church, the mission is a simple affair with a few original items on display.

SAN DIEGO

The interesting parts of San Diego are generally safe and enjoyable to explore on foot but tend to be scattered across the city and separated by petrol stations, used-car outlets and fast-food franchises. **San Diego Zoo** and **Sea World**® are attractions that few visitors want to miss. Equally worthwhile are several attractive neighbourhoods, such as **Downtown** where local efforts to revitalize a depressed area have paid off handsomely.

Downtown and the Gaslamp District ★★

Downtown San Diego is a winning blend of restored 1910s–1920s buildings and contemporary high-rises symbolizing the city's current financial strength. With the bright and busy **Horton Plaza**, corner of Broadway and Fourth Avenue, **Downtown** also has a Southern Californian rarity: a shopping mall that is open-air and not located in deepest suburbia. Beside Horton Plaza, the 16-block **Gaslamp District**, marked by red pavements, gaslamps (powered by electricity), and scores of antique shops, art galleries and restaurants, is the historical core of Downtown. It is best assessed with the Saturday guided walking tour (tel: (619) 233-4692) from the 1860 **William Heath Davis House**, 410 Island Avenue, at 11:00.

Embarcadero ★

The Embarcadero pathway links Downtown to the harbour (beside Harbor Drive), bringing views of San Diegans at play – sailing yachts, flying kites, riding mountain bikes – and passes **Seaport Village**, a conglomeration of clapboard buildings holding a mildly diverting selection of shops, cafés and restaurants.

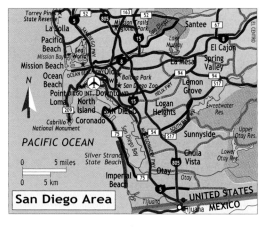

San Diego Area

Balboa Park ★★★

For the last hundred years, the 1000 acre (405ha) Balboa Park, northeast of Downtown, has been a cherished green space; when the Panama-Pacific Exposition was held here in 1915, the park acquired the first of the Spanish-Moorish buildings that now house 13 museums.

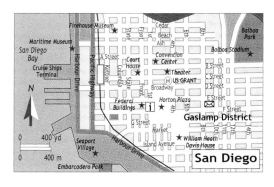

Along the lively El Prado, the **San Diego Museum of Art** (open Tuesday–Saturday 10:00–16:00; Thursday 10:00–21:00), the **Natural History Museum** (open daily 10:00–17:00) and the anthropological **Museum of Man** (open daily 10:00–16:30) are substantial but uninspiring. More enjoyable are the smaller collections: the **Timkin Museum of Art** (open Tuesday–Saturday 10:30–16:30; Sunday 13:30–16:30), with Russian icons and French tapestries, the **Museum of Photographic Arts** (open daily 10:00–17:00; Thursday until 21:00), the **San Diego History Museum** (open Wednesday–Sunday 10:00–17:00), and the **Hall of Champions** (open daily 10:00–16:30), celebrating San Diego's sporting successes. Cross the park for the **Aerospace Museum** (open daily 10:00–16:00, until 17:00 in summer) and its assortment of real and replicated flying machines, from the *Spirit of St Louis* to the **Space Shuttle**. Allow time for the **Reuben H. Fleet Space Theater and Science Center**, showing ultra-realistic documentary films on its 76ft (23m) screen (open daily 09:30–17:30).

San Diego Zoo ★★★

Adjoining Balboa Park, the renowned San Diego Zoo (open daily 09:00–17:00 or later) holds nearly 4000 species of animals, mostly in finely detailed, re-created habitats spread across 128 acres (52ha). The zoo's strengths include its primates, best seen in the pseudo-rainforest of **Gorilla Tropics**, and its 65 pigeon and dove species – although the **koalas** and **pygmy chimps** draw most human admirers.

BALBOA PARK MUSEUM TICKET

To save a little time and money, purchase a **Balboa Park Passport** from the Information Center at the **House of Hospitality** on El Prado, which is valid for a week and permits one visit to almost every museum in the park. On the first Tuesday of the month, admission to most museums is free.

The **San Diego Bay Ferry** makes
the 15-minute voyage between
B Street Pier and Coronado's
Old Ferry Landing Stage hourly
throughout most of the day.
Once landed in Coronado, the
Hotel Del Coronado is easy to
find at the end of a 20-minute
walk along Orange Avenue.
The hotel is a local landmark
for its architecture and its guest
register has included royalty,
heads of state and showbiz
stars. There is a small museum
and historical tours are given.

Above: *Whale petting
at Sea World*®.
Below: *San Diego
Mission – the first
Californian mission.*

Sea World® ★★

Its training of killer whales, dolphins and other aquatic
creatures to perform tricks has been controversial but Sea
World®, 1720 South Shores Road, continues to attract, and
usually delight, 3.5 million visitors annually (open daily
09:00 or 10:00–dusk). Besides the main shows, times of
which are given with the map on entry, Sea World® has an
enormous walk-through shark tank, a re-
created Antarctica occupied by a penguin
colony, and many other displays and exhibitions on the wonders of aquatic life.

Old Town San Diego ★

Old Town San Diego, 4 miles (6km) north
of Downtown, preserves a few of San
Diego's earliest buildings, erected here
from the early 1800s close to San Diego's
mission. They were abandoned by the
turn of the century as the town sought to
revive its flagging fortunes with a new
ocean-side location – today's Downtown.
Adobe buildings of California's Mexican
era and wood-framed shacks of the early
US days can be enjoyably viewed but
make little sense without the free self-
guided tour map distributed at the visitors' centre on California Plaza.

Mission Beach ★★

With surfers, suntans and palm trees, Mission Beach, 3 miles (5km) west of Downtown, is the Southern California of popular imagination. The **beach boardwalk** is the place to soak up the sunshine and the mood, at its most vivacious at weekends.

Coronado ★

Pretty and pricey, Coronado sits across San Diego Bay from Downtown, reached by ferry or by car on the curling Coronado Bridge. The reason for making the journey is the **Hotel Del Coronado**, 1500 Orange Avenue. Raised in the late 1800s, it quickly established a reputation as a glitterati hangout. The public rooms are lavishly furnished and there is a small museum. More informative, though, is the guided tour on Friday, Saturday and Sunday, tel: (619) 437-8788.

Above: *The Hotel del Coronado, an adored architectural landmark since the 19th century and the building that gave rise to wealthy modern-day Coronado.*

Point Loma ★

Cloaked by a swathe of pine and juniper trees, the 6 mile-long (10km) Point Loma peninsula wraps a sheltering arm around San Diego Bay. It remains in pristine condition largely because the US Navy owns and occupies much of the southern section.

At the **Cabrillo National Monument**, close to the southern tip, a statue remembers Juan Rodriguez Cabrillo, the Portuguese navigator who, in 1542, led the first European crew to drop anchor at a point near here. From this 400ft-high (122m) point are vertigo-inducing views across San Diego and south to the US-Mexico border. The **Bayside Trail** starts here, picking a downward route to numerous tidepools. The tidepools' ecology is outlined inside the nearby visitors' centre (open daily 09:00–17:00), as are the comings and goings of the California gray whale, often spotted on its December to March migration from a viewing point on the peninsula's west side.

Though smaller and less expensive than the far better known Sea World®, the **Stephen Birch Aquarium Museum**, 2300 Expedition Way, is in many ways equally enjoyable and informative. A rich array of underwater life fills the display tanks while other exhibits focus on coastal ecology; all are immeasurably useful in making sense of California's rich but threatened shoreline.
Open daily 09:00–17:00, tel: (858) 534-3474.

San Diego's Wineries

A number of reputable wineries stud the area inland from San Diego, many to be found close to I-15 (Interstate 15) in and around the town of Escondido. The largest, the **Orfila Winery**, 13455 San Pasqual Road, offers tours, tastings and picnic tables with views of vine-coated hillsides. Others include the **Bernardo Winery**, 13330 Paseo Del Verano Norte (open daily 09:00–17:00), and **the Fallbrook Winery**, 2554 Via Rancheros (open Monday–Friday 10:00–16:00; weekends by appointment; tel: (760) 728-0156).

North along the Coast

The coast north of San Diego is one of almost continuous scenic pleasure, a succession of beaches and bluffs overlooked by the colourful hillsides of the country's biggest flower-growing area. In the coastal communities, meanwhile, lurk everyone from oil company executives and retired CIA operatives to surf-crazed beach bums.

La Jolla ***

Dotted with pink stucco buildings and perched above cave-studded cliffs and tiny beaches, La Jolla is 9 miles (14km) north of Downtown San Diego. Its commercial core, known as 'the village', gathers chic boutiques, art galleries and classy eateries around the junction of Girard Avenue and Prospect Street.

Much of La Jolla's appearance results from the influence – and funding – of Ellen Scripps, whose money put much local land into public ownership and enabled architect Irving Gill to forge the town's Spanish colonial look. Scripps also established the **Museum of Contemporary Art**, 700 Prospect Street (open daily 12:00–17:00 and Thursday until 21:00), devoted to post-war painting and sculpture and featuring a strong crop of Californian artistic talent. Walk the clifftop pathway at **La Jolla Cove**, and flop into any of the public benches, decorated with elaborate wrought-iron-work, to contemplate the sheer beauty of it all.

Below: *People enjoying the view from the promenade, La Jolla.*

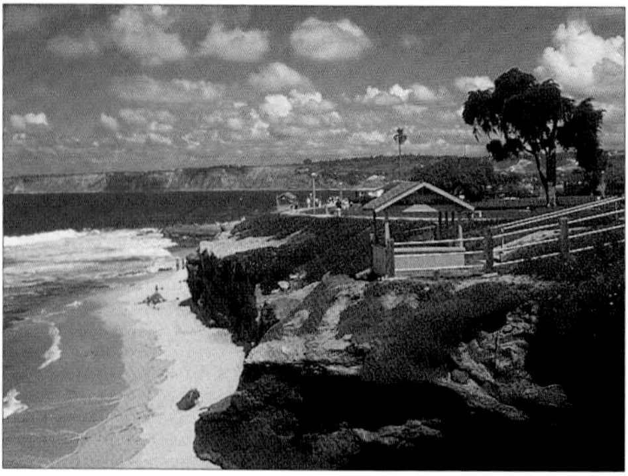

Torrey Pines State Reserve **

About 4 miles (6km) north of La Jolla, Torrey Pines Road runs through Torrey Pines State Reserve, protecting the USA's rarest form of pine tree. The 10ft-high (3m) torrey pines are twisted into angular shapes by the ocean winds. Several trails penetrate the forest and reveal exceptional ocean views.

BEST TIMES TO VISIT

There is no bad time to visit San Diego. The year-round climate is one of warm temperatures and abundant sunshine; though mornings and evenings can be cool in winter.

GETTING THERE

San Diego's **airport** has strong connections across the USA and the rest of California. Greyhound buses are frequent from Los Angeles; a few services make stops at the smaller coastal communities. Eight Amtrak **trains** arrive daily from Los Angeles. Reaching San Diego from Los Angeles by **car** is a two-hour drive on I-5.

GETTING AROUND

San Diego is feasible to explore with a combination of **public transport** and **footwork**. A **car** will save time but street parking is notoriously difficult. A car is essential, however, for exploring the north along the coast or inland.

WHERE TO STAY

LUXURY
US Grant Hotel, 326 Broadway, tel: (800) 237-5029, fax: 239-9517. Steeped in history and tradition, this downtown landmark has been pampering guests for years.

MID-RANGE
Courtyard by Marriott, 2435 Jefferson Street, tel: (619) 260-8500, fax: (619) 297-2078. On a quiet residential

street adjacent to Old Town San Diego.
Old Town Inn, 4444 Pacific Highway, San Diego, tel: 1-800 643-3025, fax: (619) 296-0524. Choice of standard room or much larger suites.

BUDGET
La Pensione, 1700 India Street, tel: (619) 236-8000, fax: (619) 236-8088. Rooms are equipped with fridges and microwaves; attractive weekly rates.

WHERE TO EAT

LUXURY
The Marine Room, 2000 Spindrift Drive, La Jolla, tel: (619) 459-7222. Very fine dining with views of the ocean.

MID-RANGE
Filippi's Pizza Grotto, 1747 India Street, tel: (619) 232-5094. Simple but delectable Italian fare.
The Prado Restaurant, House of Hospitality, Balboa Park, tel: (619) 557-9441. Eclectic globe-spanning cuisine served amid the park's finery.

BUDGET
Coronado Brewing Company, 170 Orange Avenue, Coronado, tel: (619) 437-4452. Pizzas and burgers compliment the home-brewed beers.
Old Town Mexican Café, 2489 San Diego Avenue, Old Town, tel: (609) 297-

4330. Unpretentious setting for quality Mexican food.

SHOPPING

Although the city lacks the consuming opportunities of San Francisco or Los Angeles, San Diego's **Horton Plaza**, with two major department stores, Macy's and Nordstrom, anchoring around 140 smaller shops. Much the same applies to the 160 stores of **University Town Center**, 4545 La Jolla Village Drive, which has several cinemas and an Olympic-sized skating rink.

TOURS AND EXCURSIONS

About 32km (20 miles) from San Diego lies the Mexican border city of **Tijuana**, unrepresentative of Mexico and geared to tourism but giving a brief glimpse of south-of-the border life. The **San Diego Trolley** runs from Downtown to the border crossing at **San Ysidro**, from which Tijuana is a 15-minute walk.

USEFUL CONTACTS

International Visitor Information Center, 1040 ¹⁄₃ W Broadway, daily 09:00–16:00 or 17:00, tel: (619) 236-1212, www.sandiego.org
Coronado Visitor Information Center, 1047 B Avenue, Monday–Friday 09:00–17:00, weekends 10:00–17:00, tel: (619) 437-8788.
Balboa Park Information Center, daily 09:30–16:00, tel: (619) 239-0512.

8
The Deserts

The desert regions of California are a visual record of millions of years of geological history: inland seas and lakes drying up to leave a region irregularly studded with sand dunes, salt flats, multi-coloured cliff-faces and many other remarkable features. Yet the deserts are also severe and challenging places, where powerful and haunting landscapes emerge only after crossing many miles of acutely uninteresting, scorched earth, scattered with cacti and populated only by snakes and lizards.

The desert may be unwelcoming but is by no means uninhabited. Large swathes are under military control and used for weapon research and testing. More apparent to visitors without security clearance are the huge trucks moving the produce of desert agriculture: the diverting of the Colorado River turned 8000 sq miles (20,725km²) of parched scrubland near the US-Mexico border into one of the state's most profitable farming areas.

Palm Springs is the pre-eminent town, synonymous with glamourous lifestyles but in reality a small and instantly appealing place that makes an ideal springboard for exploring **Joshua Tree National Park** and heading south to the **Salton Sea** and **Anza-Borrego Desert State Park**. The most resonant desert name, however, is **Death Valley**, best approached from Los Angeles or the Eastern Sierra. Among the world's hottest and driest places, Death Valley has sizzling temperatures and scenery to take your breath away.

DON'T MISS

*** Death Valley National Park: scorchingly hot but alive with colour and life, despite its name.
*** Joshua Tree National Park: the oddest trees you ever saw, casting their branches ever upwards.
** Palm Springs: a sybaritic desert community of world-wide fame.

Opposite: *A pale moon rise over Joshua Tree National Park.*

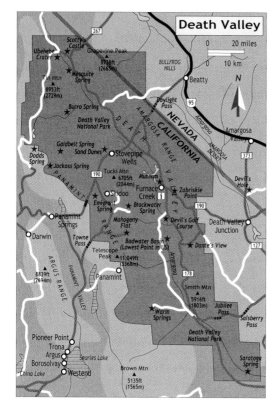

DEATH VALLEY NATIONAL PARK

The lowest, hottest and driest desert in the USA that sometimes receive only 2 inches (50mm) of rainfall a year – Death Valley nonetheless teems with life and colour: it is home to a great variety of living creatures. It is also studded with geological curiosities resulting from the evaporation of the lakes and inland seas which filled its 3000 sq miles (7772km²) through past ice ages. Plan your time carefully in Death Valley, remembering that lengthy drives separate many of the major features and that the low-lying sun of early morning or late afternoon greatly enhances the valley's natural colours.

ARTIST'S PALETTE

Artist's Drive, a signposted 9 mile-long (15km) unpaved, loop road off Highway 178 in **Death Valley** just north of the Devil's Golf Course, passes Artist's Palette. It's a cliff face where the oxidization of chemicals in the rock creates glowing shades of red, orange, yellow, green and more. For the best effect, visit just before sunset.

Furnace Creek ★

In the heart of the valley on Highway 190, the **Furnace Creek Visitor Center** (open daily 08:00–18:00) dispenses maps and information, and screens an introductory slide-show every half hour. The adjacent **museum** explains the formation of the valley and the mining of its borax, a practice which brought human settlement to the valley from the late 1800s.

Zabriskie Point ★★★

From Furnace Creek, Highway 190 climbs into the Black Mountains and after about 4 miles (6km) reaches Zabriskie Point, looking out across a stark and forbidding landscape of mustard-coloured mudhills, actually a 12-million-year-old lake bed. In the immediate background are the snow-capped peaks of the 11,000ft-high (3353m) **Panamint Mountains** – the valley's western wall.

Dante's View ★★

A turn-off 5 miles (8km) from Zabriskie Point leads to Dante's View and a stunning vista of the valley floor, 5000ft (1524m) below and around 20°F (11°C) cooler. Walk the short **Whitney View Trail** to view the USA's lowest and highest points, **Badwater** and **Mount Whitney**, simultaneously.

Devil's Golf Course ★★

About 29 miles (47km) south of Furnace Creek, Highway 178 reaches the turn-off to the Devil's Golf Course, a 200-sq-mile (518km²) expanse of saltflats – thousands of very sharp-edged hunks of near-pure salt exposed as a 600ft-deep (183m) prehistoric lake slowly evaporated.

Below: *Golden Canyon, illuminated by the sun.*

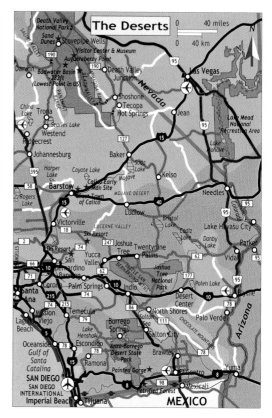

Below: A lonely path
through Zabriskie Point.

Badwater ★

The lowest point in the western hemisphere, Badwater,
4 miles (6km) on from the Devil's Golf Course on
Highway 178, lies 282ft (86m) below sea level and
consists of a brackish pool. It was named when the
owner of a mule that refused to drink from it raised a
sign saying 'bad water'. Actually, the water is drinkable
– but not at all recommended, due to its high salinity.

Stovepipe Wells Sand Dunes ★★★

Close to Stovepipe Wells, about 20 miles (32km) north
of Furnace Creek on Highway 190, Death Valley looks

exactly like a desert should, with wind-tormented sand dunes forming a 14-sq-mile (36km²) rippled, yellow blanket at the foot of towering mountains. The village of Stovepipe Wells has services and supplies, and was named in typically laconic Death Valley style when the local well was marked with a piece of stovepipe.

PALM SPRINGS AND VICINITY

An underground water basin – topped up with supplies drawn from the Colorado River – enables the rich resort of Palm Springs, and its Coachella Valley neighbours, to flourish in the heart of the **Mojave Desert**. All the towns are easily reached and explored though the region's biggest natural draw is the unmissable **Joshua Tree National Park**. A longer trip from Palm Springs crosses the **San Jacinto Mountains** to reach the bird-rich **Salton Sea** and the intensely arid **Anza-Borrego Desert**.

Above: *Not a mirage in the desert but Scotty's Castle, Death Valley's 1920s folly.*

SCOTTY'S CASTLE

Merging into the desert landscape 40 miles (64km) north of Stovepipe Wells, Scotty's Castle is an extraordinary desert folly. It's a **Spanish-style mansion** with **18 fireplaces** and a **pipe organ** built in 1924 for a wealthy Chicago businessman but named for Death Valley Scotty, a local character with a dubious reputation. Guided tours reveal the intrigue-laced history of the castle.

Above: *An oasis in the desert, Palm Springs.*

AIR MUSEUM

A collection of well-preserved World War II combat aircraft and assorted exhibits form the Palm Springs Air Museum, open daily 10:00–17:00, close to the local airport off Hwy-111.

AERIAL TRAMWAY

The Palm Springs Aerial Tramway carries skiers 6000ft (1829m) up onto the snow-coated slopes of the **San Jacinto Mountains**. In summer, when the slopes are bare, the tramway continues in operation, putting walkers and picnickers in reach of the mountain's sub-alpine landscapes and views far across the **Coachella Valley**.

Palm Springs ★★

An oasis of swimming pools and about a hundred golf courses, Palm Springs began climbing the social ladder from the 1930s, when a handful of Hollywood celebrities discovered its blue skies, clean air and warm winters, and snapped up low-priced land to build opulent homes. Though its fame may be vast, Palm Springs is small and easy to explore. Away from the chic boutiques and art galleries dotted along **Palm Canyon Drive**, however, there is little specifically to see. **Moorten Botanical Garden**, 1701 S Palm Canyon Drive (open Monday–Saturday 09:00–16:30; Sunday 10:00–16:00; closed in summer), with a large gathering of desert flora, and the **Art Museum**, 101 Museum Drive (open Tuesday, Wednesday, Friday–Sunday 10:00–17:00; Thursday 12:00–20:00; closed in summer), with a small but commendable permanent stock of contemporary art and good quality travelling exhibitions. Just south of the town, amid waterfalls, **Indian Canyons** hold the country's densest concentration of palm trees.

Coachella Valley ★★

Palm Springs is just one of several communities lining the Coachella Valley on Highway 111, and its wealth pales in comparison with that of **Rancho Mirage**, immediately east, where the average home is a mini-fortress.

Frank Sinatra and Bob Hope are just two of the town's residents with streets named after them. By contrast, **Indio**, on the valley's eastern edge, is a simple farming town whose agricultural yield includes the world's biggest crop of dates. Worth $20 million annually, the date harvest is celebrated by February's **National Date Festival**, with ostrich and camel races, and all the dates you could want to eat.

Joshua Tree National Park ★★★

At sunrise or sunset, when the sun paints huge granite monoliths in red-orange hues and the stumpy branches of thousands of Joshua trees cast long shadows, there are few more captivating natural sights than **Joshua Tree National Park**. It is situated approximately 20 miles (32km) northeast of the **Coachella Valley** but is best approached via Highway 62, using the entrance immediately east of Twentynine Palms. The trees, giant yuccas, growing up to 50ft (15m), were named by 19th-century Mormon travellers who matched them to a passage in the Book of Joshua and believed the branches to be showing the route ahead. The largest of the trees and the best of the scenery

> **JUMPING CACTUS**
>
> Found at **Joshua Tree National Park's Cholla Cactus Garden**, the jumping cholla is a member of the *Opuntia cacti* family, distinguished by its dark trunk and the bundles of very thin spines. Once these spines attach themselves to human skin, they are extremely difficult to shake off and very irritating to the skin.

Below: *Joshua Tree National Park.*

Above: *The extreme dryness of the Anza-Borrego Desert is overwhelming.*

is to be seen around **Covington Flats** in the western section of the 878-sq-miles (2274km²) national monument.

Salton Sea ★★

The Salton Sea is reached from the Coachella Valley on highways 86 or 111, which branch south off I-10 at Indio. The Salton Sea developed from an unforeseen and unintentional combination of natural and human circumstances in 1905, when the **Colorado River** spilled over the canals built to divert it to Southern California's farmlands and created an inland sea filling 340 sq miles (881km²).

The sea's salinity – evaporation has left it 10% saltier than the Pacific Ocean – brings water-sports enthusiasts and anglers to the campsites and jetties on the north and east sides. Meanwhile, the saltwater marshes and freshwater ponds on the southern edge have become an important stopover for migrating waterfowl and a nesting ground for about 200 bird species. From autumn to spring, snowy egrets, great blue herons and green-winged teals are among the creatures keeping amateur ornithologists gazing through binoculars for hours.

Anza-Borrego Desert State Park ★

This is the USA's largest state park and lies just west of the Salton Sea on highways 22 and 78. Some of the park's most powerful and desolate terrain can be admired from a dirt road leading from Highway 22 to a lookout point across the **Borrego Badlands**, a huge expanse of barren mudflats, once a lake bed but pushed upwards and eroded over thousands of years by the wind. Highway 22 leads into **Borrego Springs**, irrigated by natural springs and the park's centre of population – a popular winter home for San Diegans – with an excellent visitors' centre. Open daily 09:00–17:00; weekends only June–September.

The Deserts at a Glance

BEST TIMES TO VISIT

Desert touring is only sensible between **autumn** and **spring**; even then you should be prepared for daytime temperatures reaching 90°F (32°C). **Palm Springs** can be visited year-round, though many museums and visitor services are closed during the summer.

GETTING THERE

Flights are frequent into Palm Springs from other Californian and US cities. Greyhound **buses** from Los Angeles run to Palm Springs several times daily; Amtrak **trains** on the Sunset Limited route call three times weekly. By **car**, Death Valley can be reached from the Eastern Sierra on Highway 190, which branches off Highway 395 at Olancha and can also be joined from Highway 136 from Lone Pine. Palm Springs and the Coachella are a two- to three-hour drive west of Los Angeles on I-10 and a similar distance from San Diego, either with I-15 (Interstate) or the slower but more scenic mountain roads.

GETTING AROUND

A very limited bus service operates in Palm Springs and the Coachella Valley but any further desert travel requires a car.

WHERE TO STAY

Death Valley
LUXURY
Furnace Creek Inn and Ranch, Furnace Creek; tel: (760) 786-

2345; fax: (760) 786-2514. Fully equipped inn.

Palm Springs and Vicinity
LUXURY
Ingleside Inn, 200 W Ramon Road, Palm Springs; tel: (760) 325-0046; fax: (760) 325-0710.

MID-RANGE
Desert Riviera Inn, 610 E Palm Canyon Drive, Palm Springs, tel: (760) 327-5314, fax: (760) 322-9467. Nice rooms, pool and good location.

BUDGET
Motel 6, 666 S Palm Canyon Drive, tel: (760) 324-4200, fax: (760) 324-9827. Nationwide chain with the lowest rates in town.

WHERE TO EAT

Death Valley
MID-RANGE
Furnace Creek Ranch, many eateries, offering burgers to gourmet food.

Palm Springs and Vicinity
LUXURY
Melvyn's Ingleside Inn, 200 W Ramon Road, Palm Springs; tel: (760) 325-2323. Rare is the socialite not

acquainted with this very elegant restaurant and its European-slanted menu.

MID-RANGE
Café Italia, 2500 N Palm Canyon Drive, Palm Springs, tel: (760) 864-1833. Good Italian fare.

BUDGET
Sherman's Deli, 401 E Tahquitz Canyon Way, Palm Springs, tel: (760) 325-1199. Reliable New York-style deli and bakery.

USEFUL CONTACTS

Death Valley Furnace Creek Visitor Center; tel: (760) 786-2331.
Palm Springs Visitor Information Center, 2781 N Palm Canyon Drive; tel: (760) 778-8418.
Anza-Borrego Desert State Park; tel: (760) 767-4684.
Joshua Tree National Park, tel: (760) 367-7511.
Borrego Springs Visitor Information Center; 622 Palm Canyon Drive; tel: (760) 767-5311.
California Desert Information Center, junction of Barstow Road and I-15, tel: (760) 252-6060.

DEATH VALLEY	J	F	M	A	M	J	J	A	S	O	N	D
AVERAGE TEMP. °C	11	13	16	22	27	31	35	37	33	25	15	10
AVERAGE TEMP. °F	52	55	61	71	81	88	95	99	91	77	59	50
DAYS OF RAINFALL	1	1	2	1	1	1	1	1	1	1	1	2
RAINFALL mm	6	5	6	6	8	8	11	11	8	4	5	3
RAINFALL in	0.2	0.2	0.2	0.2	0.3	0.3	0.4	0.4	0.3	0.2	0.2	0.1

Travel Tips

Tourist Information

As much information as anyone needs is available from the various convention and visitors bureaux and chambers of commerce throughout California, while the **California Office of Tourism** can provide material on the state in general: P. O. Box 1499, Sacramento, CA 95812-1499; tel: (916) 444-4429 or toll-free 1-800 862-2543 (in the US and Canada). Their website, www.visit california.com, is very comprehensive.

Entry Requirements

Regulations regarding entry to the US have tightened considerably in recent years and are subject to sudden change. Currently, in addition to a full passport, all visitors need either a US Visa or be traveling from a visa-waiver country (listed on the website) with a machine-readable passport, and those issued after 26 October 2006 require an integrated chip with information from the data page (usually known as an 'e-passport'), though there are certain exceptions depending on

when the passport was issued and the form of photo. The latest details can be checked at the relevant section of the U.S. Department of State website: http://travel.state.gov/visa Arrivals should be able to provide details of where they are intending to stay and show they have sufficient funds to last the duration of their visit.

Customs

Duty free allowances for arrivals aged 21 and over include one litre of alcoholic spirits or wine, 200 cigarettes or 100 cigars, and up to three gifts of a total not exceeding $800. Among items not permitted are meat, fruit, plants, chocolate liqueurs and lottery tickets. Medications bought over the counter in other countries may be prescription only in the USA.

Health Requirements

Provided travellers arrive from safe areas, no inoculations are required or recommended for entry into the USA.

Insurance

Insurance is not compulsory but is necessary to safeguard

against potentially astronomical medical bills, as well as the usual recompense in respect of lost or stolen luggage and delayed travel.

Getting There

By Air: The national airlines of many countries have non-stop services to LA and, usually slightly less frequently, to San Francisco. These cities are California's major air hubs but all of the state's regional airports are served by US domestic carriers, and some by international ones.

By Road: California is a long drive from anywhere in the USA or Canada and motorists will also have to cross deserts or mountain ranges before reaching the major cities of the Californian coast. Nonetheless, car enthusiasts who shun widely advertised and often money-saving flight-and-car-rental deals will find themselves entering California on I-5 (Interstate highway) from Oregon, I-80 from northern Nevada, or I-10, I-15 or I-140 from the Southwest states.

By Rail: Discount fares periodically offered by Amtrak, the US rail passenger operator,

can make travelling to
California by train relatively
inexpensive, but time-consum-
ing. Several daily trains operate on different routes between
Chicago and Los Angeles, and
there is a daily service from
Chicago to San Francisco. Los
Angeles and San Francisco
can also be reached on a daily
service from Vancouver which
makes stops in Washington
and Oregon.

What to Pack
On the southern coast, light,
cotton clothing is ideal for day
wear although pack a jacket or
sweater for the cool evenings.
Further north, cooler conditions dictate warmer clothing
be on hand. In the mountains
and far north, expect cool conditions even in summer; in the
desert, expect warm conditions even in winter. Carry
walking shoes for exploring
the state and national parks;
sunscreen is essential for
deserts, beaches and mountains. Restaurant dress is generally casual; only the most
formal dining places insist on
elegant attire.

Money Matters
Banks: Monday–Friday 9:00–
17:00 or 17:30, with some
branches open on Saturdays.
Currency: US currency
includes the notes: $100, $50,
$20, $10, $5 and $1; and the
variously sized coins: 25c (a
'quarter'), 10c (a 'dime'), 5c
(a 'nickel') and 1c (a 'penny').
Currency exchange: Other
than small amounts of cash,
much the best way to carry
money is as US dollar trav-

ellers cheques, which can be
used like cash (sign the
cheque then wait for your
change) in hotels, restaurants
and major larger shops. Most
hotel cashiers will also
exchange US travellers
cheques for cash. It is unusual
for US dollar travellers
cheques to be cashed in a
bank and doing so will require
ID and may incur a commis-
sion fee. Obtain your cheques
before leaving home; changing foreign currency, or foreign currency travellers
cheques, in California is an
ordeal best avoided. If it cannot be avoided, foreign currency travellers cheques and
currency may be exchanged at
major banks and exchange
bureaux: *Thomas Cook* and
American Express are the
biggest names.
Credit cards: All major credit
cards are widely accepted and
commonly used; most motels
and hotels will take a credit
card imprint on arrival and
deduct charges from this
unless requested otherwise.
Without a credit card, payment for the first night, at least,
must be made on arrival.
Tipping: Provided you receive
satisfactory service, tipping is
widespread and expected. In a
restaurant or taxi tip 15%–20%
of the total bill; for a helpful
hotel porter give $1 per bag.
Service charges: Some cities
have a hotel tax which, added
to other local taxes, can add
about 12% to a room's price.
State sales tax: At least 7.25%
is added to the marked price
of everything purchased; subject to local variations.

Accommodation
California excels at providing
quality accommodation in all
price ranges, from plain and
simple **motels** – the rooms
invariably equipped with dou-
ble bed, colour TV, telephone
and bathroom – to **luxury
resorts** where in-room jacuzzis
and fax machines are taken for
granted. In addition, there are
a growing number of **bed-and-
breakfast** inns. These are often
atmospheric, converted
Victorian homes. Advance
booking is advisable.

Eating Out
See **At a Glance**, at the end
of every chapter.

Transport
By Air: Many regional airlines
operate within California and
have discounted fares which
are advertised locally. These
usually involve travelling as a
stand-by passenger (without
confirmed reservation but able
to board when a seat is available) which can be inconve-
nient but can save money.
Also worth looking out for
are flight and hotel packages
to resorts such as Lake Tahoe
and Palm Springs from other
Californian cities.
By Road: As in the rest of
the USA, Interstate Highways
(odd numbers generally run
north–south; even numbers
east–west) provide swift connections over long distances
while a comprehensive network of state highways, and a
few smaller county roads, link
California's cities, towns and
points of interest. The roads
range from the narrow but

scenic Highway 1 along the coast, to the multi-lane freeways bisecting the heart of Los Angeles. **The American Automobile Association** (AAA, tel: toll-free 1-800 222-4357), based at 1000 AAA Drive, Heathrow, FL 32746, provide free maps and assistance to AA members of other countries.

Car hire: All major car rental firms have offices throughout the state and at its airports. To rent, a full driving licence is all that is required for citizens of most countries. Charges rise for drivers under 25; drivers under 21 will rarely be able to rent. Payment should be made by credit card; otherwise a sizeable deposit will be needed in cash or travellers cheques. International arrivals may find there are savings to be made by booking a car in advance of landing. Insurance is usually included in the rental price (but ask to be sure). Collision or Loss Damage Waiver (CDW or LDW), which otherwise costs around $10–15 a day is important. Without CDW, renters will be liable for any damage incurred to the rental car. Within the USA, most major car rental companies can be reached on toll-free numbers: **Avis**, tel: 1-800 331-1212. **Budget**, tel: 1-800 527-0700. **Dollar**, tel: 1-800 800-4000. **Hertz**, tel: 1-800 654-3131. **National**, tel: 1-800 227-7368. **Thrifty**, tel: 1-800 847-4389.

Road rules and signs: On interstates, the main fast-moving multi-lane routes across the state, there is a marked speed limit of 55mph (89kph) or 65mph (105kph) and some sections may have signposted minimum speeds. Although speed limits are commonly exceeded, on-the-spot fines can be imposed for doing so. Lower speed limits are signposted in towns and cities. Driving with an open alcohol container is an offence, regardless of whether or not the driver has been drinking; any measurable alcohol in a driver's blood constitutes drunk driving and is a serious offence.

Petrol: Compared to most countries, petrol is extremely cheap and petrol stations are plentiful in all but the most remote areas. Unless requested otherwise, rental cars will have automatic transmission.

Trains: Anti-pollution initiatives have led to increased passenger services on California's few rail passenger routes, though many towns are several hours by road from the nearest station and passengers are conveyed to the trains by bus. As yet, however, rail travel is more of a novelty than a practical means of getting about though there are some scenic routes, such as the Coastal Starlight between Los Angeles and San Francisco. All services are run by **Amtrak**, tel: 1-800 USA RAIL.

Taxis: Taxi ranks exist at some airports and a few major hotels, and cabs can also be hailed in city streets, but it is more common to phone for one: scores of local taxi firms are listed in *Yellow Pages*. Average taxi fares are around $2 plus $1.50–1.70 for each mile (1.6km) travelled. Taxis can also charge for being stuck in traffic, a likely occurrence during city rush hours.

Buses: Greyhound buses (tel: 1-800 231-2222) provide services across California but are only at all frequent and reliable between San Francisco, Sacramento, Los Angeles and San Diego. Many parts of the state are far from Greyhound routes or are only served by a once-daily service. Where several communities lie in close proximity, such as the Monterey Peninsula, local buses can be a quicker and inexpensive means of getting around although local services are reduced or non-existent at weekends and evenings.

Business Hours

The Californian business day generally begins at 08:00 or 09:00 and ends at 16:00 or 17:00. Bank hours are Monday to Friday from 09:00–17:00 or 17:30, with some branches open on Saturdays. Typical shop hours are weekdays and Saturdays 09:00 or 10:00 to 17:00 or 18:00. Department stores and shops in popular tourist areas are likely to keep longer hours and may be open on Sundays.

Time Difference

Time is 8hrs behind GMT. California uses Pacific Standard Time: 3 hours behind the US East Coast, 8 hours behind the UK, 9 hours behind the rest of Western Europe, and 16–18 hours behind Australia. The time difference may vary by an hour during the Daylight Saving Time period, in effect from the first Sunday in April to the last Sunday in October.

Communications

Post: Postal services are swift and reliable. Stamps are available from post offices and, more expensively, from vending machines in hotels. Post offices in major cities generally open Monday to Friday from 08:00–18:00 and on Saturdays from 08:00–13:00. Post office locations are given in phone books.

Telephones: Public telephones are easy to find. Local calls typically cost 30–45c (depending on the local phone company); insert coins before dialling (no change given). Calls from hotel room phones are liable to be much more expensive than those made on a public phone, though some motels offer free local calls from rooms. Many businesses can be called on toll-free numbers (prefixed 1-800, 866, 1-877, 1-8 or 1-888), which

do not require any coins to be inserted. Some hotels, however, charge for toll-free calls made from rooms. Businesses may also make use of US telephones' letter and number dial to express their telephone number: such as the rail service, **Amtrak,** with toll-free tel: 1-800 USA-RAIL.

Fax: Some shops have fax machines – marked by a large sign outside – for public use, operated by a credit card. Most accommodations have fax machines and will send a fax on guests' behalf though many charge (and some charge steeply) for this. Some hotels also charge for receiving faxes on guests' behalf.

Electricity

The US electrical supply is 110 volts (60 cycles) and appliances use two-prong plugs. Appliances designed for other voltages can only be used with an adapter. Many electrical goods, such as computers, VCRs and CD players, are often cheaper in the USA than elsewhere but may be unus-

able in other countries; check before buying. DVDs bought in the US are likely to be region coded, so it may not play elsewhere without the DVD player being re-coded. Software, though, is useable on any suitable computer.

Weights and Measures

The USA uses the Imperial system of weights and measures, though the US gallon and pint are each roughly 80% of their Imperial counterparts.

Health Precautions

Unless you are undertaking a major expedition into sparsely populated areas, such as desert (note the general tips for desert travel given on page 114) or mountain regions, no particular health precautions are necessary for travel in California. Nonetheless, always seek the advice of park rangers before entering wild areas. In mountains and foothills, remember that the high altitudes will leave you short of breath after even light exertion. Any dizziness may be the first sign of altitude sickness and if this occurs you should rest and seek medical help.

Health Services

High standards and high costs are the main traits of California's health services and visitors are strongly advised to be adequately insured for even minor medical treatment. Major cities have at least one hospital with a 24-hour casualty department; details in the phone book or **call: 911**.

CONVERSION CHART

From	To	Multiply By
Millimetres	Inches	0.0394
Metres	Yards	1.0936
Metres	Feet	3.281
Kilometres	Miles	0.6214
Square kilometres	Square miles	0.386
Hectares	Acres	2.471
Litres	Pints	1.760
Kilograms	Pounds	2.205
Tonnes	Tons	0.984

To convert Celsius to Fahrenheit: x 9 ÷ 5 + 32

For non-emergency need of a doctor or dentist, look under '**Physicians and Surgeons**' or '**Dentists**' in the *Yellow Pages*. Again, even the most minor treatment can be very costly. Pharmacies are plentiful but many drugs available elsewhere require a prescription in the USA and may be known by different names. If intending to buy prescription drugs while in California, you will need a note from your own doctor. Major cities and towns have late-night pharmacies; details are given in local phone books and local newspapers.

Personal Safety
Travel anywhere in California is generally safe and enjoyable though visitors should heed common sense precautions. When walking in cities, do so purposefully and consult a map only out of public view. Avoid walking into alleyways and obviously run-down areas.

When driving, plan your route carefully. In cities use freeways whenever possible. Do not stop to assist an apparently broken-down vehicle but report the incident to the **California Highway Patrol** (CHP) from the next phone. Rental cars will have a number prominently displayed to call if the car breaks down in a busy locality.

Emergencies
Fire, police or ambulance; tel: **911**. No money required. Each city also has emergency numbers and help lines; the local phone book has a list.

PUBLIC HOLIDAYS

1 January •
New Year's Day
third Monday in January •
Martin Luther King's Birthday
third Monday in February •
President's Day
nearest Mon or Fri to 31 March • Cesar Chavez Day
25 May •
Memorial Day
4 July •
Independence Day
first Monday in September •
Labor Day,
second Monday in October •
Columbus Day
November 11 •
Veteran's Day
fourth Thursday in November •
Thanksgiving Day
December 25 •
Christmas Day
Good Friday
is a half-day holiday
and
Easter Monday
is a full day holiday

Festivals
Around 5000 festivals are celebrated annually throughout California. Most of these are local events advertised in newspapers and they include **Indio's Date Festival** and **Bodega Bay's Bathtub Race**. California's biggest festivals, however, are those celebrated throughout the USA and two can bring considerable disruption to travel plans. On July 4, **Independence Day** is marked by a day-long holiday, fireworks, processions and other

special events. On the last Thursday in November, **Thanksgiving** is a family occasion, when relatives get together over a turkey dinner to commemorate the first successful harvest of the Pilgrim Fathers, who landed in New England in 1620. Another nationwide event, though not a public holiday, is October 31, **Halloween**. Everywhere are pumpkin lamps, special events and people striding about in outlandish costumes though the practice of children knocking on strangers' doors asking for 'trick or treat' is no more.

GOOD READING

• Banham, Reyner (1986) *Los Angeles: The Architecture of Four Ecologies*. Penguin.
• Brogan, Hugh (1985) *The Penguin History of the United States of America*. Penguin.
• Chandler, Raymond (1983). *The Chandler Collections Vols 1 & 2*. Picador.
• Davis, Mike (1990) *City of Quartz: Excavating the Future in Los Angeles*. Verso.
• Dunlop, Carol (1982) *California People*. P. Smith.
• Ellroy, James (1988) *The Black Dahlia*. Mysterious.
• Hart, James D. (1987) *A Companion to California*. University of California Press.
• Iacopi, Robert (1978) *Earthquake Country: How and Why Earthquakes Happen in California*. Sunset.
• Seth, Vikram (1986) *The Golden Gate*. Faber & Faber.
• Tan, Amy (1989) *The Joy Luck Club*. Minerva.

INDEX